Deaf & Sober
Journeys Through Recovery

Deaf & Sober
Journeys Through Recovery

Betty G. Miller, Ed.D., C.A.D.C.

National Association of the Deaf
Silver Spring, Maryland

National Association of the Deaf Publications
814 Thayer Avenue, Silver Spring, MD 20910-4500 • *www.nad.org*

© 1998 by National Association of the Deaf. All rights reserved. No part of this publication may be used or reproduced without written permission from the National Association of the Deaf.

Printed in the United States of America
ISBN 0-913072-86-9

Illustrations © 1998 by Betty G. Miller
Cover and book design by Nancy Creighton

To all recovering deaf alcoholics and addicts who have determination, courage and a brave heart, remaining sober in spite of all barriers and access issues.

Table of Contents

Foreword xi

I am Grateful xiii

Introduction xvii

Challenges: Who Are the Deaf Substance Abusers? 1

Kate's Story 3 • Deaf Persons who have Professional Careers 5 • Allison 5 • The Disease Concept and Terminology 8 • Deaf Substance Abusers 9 • Education 12 • Deaf Adults Who are Educationally Retarded 12 • Growing Up Dependent 13 • The Impact of Being Deaf 14 • Deafened 14 • Culturally Deaf People 17 • Hard of Hearing 17 • Brynn's Story 18 • Allen's Story 21 • Putting All Recovering Deaf People in One Program 22 • Terry, Wilbur, and Joe 23 • Jack 24

The Deaf Community, ASL, and Deaf Culture:
   Impact on Recovering Deaf People 27

Elizabeth's Story 27 • The Deaf Community 28 • American Sign Language 30 • Perspectives on Culture and Deaf Culture 32 • Deaf Culture 32 • Views on Deaf Culture 32 • David 34 • Cultural Confusion/Identity Confusion 35 • Language, Personal, and Social Identities 37 • Cultural Obstacles to Recovery 39 • The Trust-Mistrust Phenomenon 40 • Community Reentry 42 • Minority Deaf People in Recovery 44 • An African-American Deaf Person in Recovery 44 • Gay and Lesbian Deaf People in Recovery 46 • Deaf Women and Addiction 47 • Making Transitions in the Process of Early Recovery 49 • Deaf Role Models 50 • Image 52

Betty G. Miller

Treatment Programs: Deaf Units 55
Jeanne and Ben 55 • Assessment by Deaf Addiction Counselors 56 • Types of Alcohol and Drug Treatment Programs 57 • Intake 59 • A Social Model Recovery Program of Deaf and Hard of Hearing People 64

Aftercare and Beyond 67
Jon's Story 67 • What is Aftercare? 68 • Early Stages of Recovery 69 • Self-Concept Building Skills 69 • Decision Making Skills 70 • Drug Differentiation Skills 71 • Stress Management Skills 73 • Jean's Story 74 • Relationship Building Skills 75 • Alice 75 • Extended Family Members 77 • Paul and Jim 78 • Help Seeking Skills 79 • Melvin 80 • Asking for Help from AA and Other 12 Step Meetings 81 • Kevin 83 • Use of a Telephone Relay Service 83 • Providing Support 83 • Jack 84 • Coping Skills 84 • Veronica 84 • Veronica's Experience in Learning to Cope at Work 85 • Recreational Activities as a Coping Skill 86 • Learning Coping Skills at 12 Step Meetings 87 • Sexuality and Intimacy 88 • Sexual Identity and Sexual Behavior 89 • Susan 89 • George 89 • Denise 90 • Intimacy 90 • Empowerment as Part of the Recovery Process 91

Alcoholics Anonymous, Its Twelve Steps and Twelve Traditions 95
Helen's Story 95 • Alcoholics Anonymous 96 • AA Sponsors 98 • Deaf 12 Step Meetings 99 • Working the 12 Steps 100 • An Interview with a Deaf Member of AA 107 • The Twelve Traditions 111 • Use of Twelve Traditions in Deaf Meetings 111 • Deaf Adult Children of Alcoholics: Who are They? 116 • Deaf Al-Anon Members: Who are They? 118

Deaf Staff in Substance Abuse Treatment Programs 121
Carla's Story 121 • Why Deaf Staff? 123 • Staff Issues 124 • Co-Dependency and Enabling 124 • Co-Dependency and the Deaf Community 125 • Dave 126 • Dual Relationships 127 • Bill 129 • Co-dependency and Hearing Staff 130 • Involving a Third Party (a Sign Language Interpreter) in Therapy 131 • Conflicts

Between Deaf and Hearing Staff 132 • Burnout 134 • Peter 134 • Marybeth 136 • Interpreters for Deaf Staff 137

Interpreting Issues 139
Jennifer's Story 139 • Julie: A Hearing AA Member's Story 140 • The Interpreter's Role 141 • Selecting a Certified Interpreter 143 • Code of Ethics 144 • Confidentiality 144 • Interpreting Issues in Treatment and AA Settings 145 • Interpreting Issues in Treatment Programs 147 • Volunteer Interpreters 149 • Paid Interpreters 150 • Funding for Interpreting Services 151 • Should AA Groups Share the Costs of Interpreting Services? 152 • Need for Boundaries 154 • Interpreter as Barrier 155 • Recovering Interpreters 156

Access Laws: Section 504 and ADA 159
Dr. Betty G. Miller, Advocate 159 • Advocacy 160 • Section 504 161 • The Americans with Disabilities Act of 1990 162 • Organizing 164 • Advocacy and Empowerment 165 • Carl 166

Friends, Family, and Spirituality 169
Letting Friends Know 170 • Anonymous 171 • Service Providers 172 • Professional Deaf People in Recovery 173 • Spirituality 174 • Amanda's Story 174 • Higher Power 176

Appendix A: The Twelve Steps 179
Appendix B: The Twelve Traditions 181
Appendix C: Thirteen Statements of Acceptance
   for Deaf Persons 183
Glossary of Key Terms 185
Bibliography 189
Index 193

Foreword

The 18th century writer, poet, and philosopher, Ralph Waldo Emerson, referring to a wounded but resilient friend who was reclaiming his life, said, "...like the wounded oyster, he mends his shell with a pearl."

This long awaited book by Dr. Betty G. Miller, my friend and mentor, is a pearl. I am honored beyond measure that Betty asked me to introduce her book to you.

It is the story of remarkable deaf artist on a journey to find her freedom, her integrity, her heart, and her potential. It is the story of a long march from hell to extraordinariness as the preeminent counselor to deaf people with alcohol and drug addiction. It is a window to understanding the unique challenges and experiences of deaf people with addiction. It is a lifeline to deaf people with addiction, their loved ones, and their helpers. It is a guidebook for hopefulness and recovery.

I was introduced to Betty Miller through her art long before I met her. The clear, powerful lines. The provocative images. So many deaf friends display her work in their homes and workplaces. They display her work, not just because she is a deaf artist, but because her art captures the feelings, the passions, and the sensibilities of deaf people.

That same gift was later so apparent to me in Betty's tireless counseling and advocacy work with Washington, DC's poorest Black deaf addicts. She was an oasis for these most invisible members of society, deaf addicts whose lives had collapsed. Behind a smile that could melt

Betty G. Miller

snow, Betty Miller was determined to find a place at the table for everyone. Her tireless work reflected the words of the poet, W.H. Auden, who said, "We must squeeze the slave out of ourselves, drop by drop." I recall telling generations of book-weary deaf and hearing Gallaudet University counseling graduate students assigned to work with Betty to simply open their hearts to her message and her methods.

Dr. Betty Miller has brought her message about the recovery of deaf addicts to workshop audiences across the country for many years. Good fortune made it possible for Professor Fran White and me to collaborate with Betty on several unique graduate Gallaudet University courses on "Counseling Deaf Addicts." We also worked with Betty to produce a number of national conferences, monographs, and videos on drug abuse prevention with deaf children. Now, through this book, you can learn what we learned from Dr. Betty Miller about addiction and recovery in the Deaf community. This book represents a new canvas for Betty Miller, each chapter painted with a palette of honesty, wisdom, experience, and devotion to the Deaf community.

> William P. McCrone, Ed.D., J.D.
> Professor of Counseling
> Dean, School of Education & Human Services
> Gallaudet University
> Washington, DC

I am Grateful

It has been a privilege that in the past 20 years of my career as an addiction counselor and consultant, I have been able to learn, understand, experience and be trusted by deaf people who are in recovery. I am deeply grateful, and appreciate that they shared with me their experience, strength and hope, including some who shared their professional experiences as deaf counselors.

I am equally grateful for these sites which provided support and/or spaces for my work with deaf people: St. Joseph Hospital, Addiction Treatment Program Unit, Burbank, CA; Greater Los Angeles Council of the Deaf, CA; Family Services Center, Torrance, CA; Deafpride, Inc., Washington, DC, and the Mental Health Center, Gallaudet University, Washington, DC.

I have been very fortunate to have had the opportunity to work with experienced writers who added to the development of this book and encouraged my growth as a writer during the past five years: editorial work by Judith Treesburg, Mary Ellen Carew, Kathy Wood, and Dawn Bradley, along with comments and expert advice from Dr. Barbara M. Kannapell, Dr. Fran White, Sarah Geer, and Dr. William McCrone. Thanks, also to Bill Stifter, who proofread this book. All errors, however, remain my own.

Nancy Creighton has been my emotional and spiritual support from the very beginning of my work with the manuscript, both at home and at work. This was essential for the development, and the

Betty G. Miller

"keep on keeping on" spirit needed to get this book published. Also special to me is Natalie Case, who has given me ongoing emotional and spiritual support since the beginning of my sobriety. For these people I am always grateful.

My special thanks go to Nancy J. Bloch and Anita B. Farb of the National Association of the Deaf for their support and faith in having this book published.

Special thanks to all my recovering friends and clients, both deaf and hearing, who shared their experience, strength, and hope as well as giving of their support and knowledge — they made this book happen.

Goddess bless them all. Without them, this book would not be possible, plus the fact that I was, by the grace of Goddess, able to remain sober the past 27 years. It is this quality (not quantity) of sobriety that made me what I am today.

Introduction

Recovering Deaf People

In the past several years, treatment programs for deaf persons in need of assistance to become sober have emerged in increasing numbers in many states. Such programs provide access for deaf people to obtain quality inpatient and outpatient treatment. Yet after completing these programs, deaf people often relapse when they return to their deaf communities.

Many of these deaf people grew up isolated. They might be separated by labels applied to them such as "oralists," "hearing deaf," "deaf-deaf," and related labels. In response to the pressures exerted by "normal" society, they learned to behave like hearing people and fit themselves into the hearing world. They were taught by their families, caregivers, and educators to stand on their own and be independent. Yet, they became dependent, not only on alcohol and drugs, but also on people, places and things. The symptoms of their underlying problems would often intensify if they were members of a minority group as well as deaf.

On a daily basis, deaf people are often confronted with oppression and low expectations in both the hearing and deaf worlds, and experience conflicting attitudes among themselves within their deaf communities. For example, there are often love/hate relationships with sign language interpreters due to confidentiality and trust issues. There are ambivalent feelings about being deaf or hard of hearing, and ambivalence in relationships with professional helpers (both deaf and hearing). Deaf people are told that they can do anything with their lives, but often by those people who "know what is best for them," whom they may not feel are sincere.

Deaf people may be confused by the differences between their own perceptions, and hearing people's perceptions, of the Deaf World. There are questions about control issues among the members of the deaf community. Most deaf people, especially those who became alcoholics and addicts, grew up feeling powerless. In fact, low self-esteem is one of the most painful feelings among deaf people.

Learning how to live without abusing substances is always difficult, and a slow process. Because of their addictive nature, it takes an enormously long time for recovering persons to make changes in their attitudes and behaviors. Yet these changes are essential to be able to deal with everyday relationships at work and at home, while at the same time maintaining sobriety.

Many resources, such as recovery-oriented literature, videotapes, workshops, and sponsors are not readily available or accessible to deaf people. Throughout the country, there are very few, if any, opportunities to provide education during aftercare for recovering deaf persons.

Perhaps it is now time for the deaf community to take more responsibility to empower recovering deaf persons to ensure their rights. The right to be educated. The right to have access to the tools necessary to cope with life without drugs. The right to be trained to deal with difficult decisions and life choices. The right to be themselves. To do so, recovering deaf people, along with friends and family members, must work together and learn about the social and political realities of being deaf in this country.

It is true that there have been several substance abuse conferences in the past few years, which offered training and workshops that were enlightening for the few recovering deaf persons who attended. But most of the training and workshops were targeted to professionals who work with deaf people in recovery.

There are some issues that deaf persons have to face during their early stages of recovery. Many are not aware of the pain they have been suppressing by their use of alcohol and drugs. The fictitious stories with fictitious names in the book are based on many recovering deaf people's experiences as they went through the process of recovery. If someone feels one of these stories is similar to their own, please bear in mind that these stories are not intended to identify specific people. They are fictitious — but also very, very common to what all people in recovery experience. Although we are individual people, with different experiences, there is no such thing as being truly unique, whether we are deaf or hearing. So many of our experiences, and so many of our stories, are universal.

With appropriate training and education, and with the help of a 12 Step program, recovering deaf people can address their misdirected behavior issues immediately, during the early part of their recovery. Usually, this education occurs during the inpatient or outpatient treatment programs as part of the recovery process, prior to aftercare. This learning process usually takes time, and for many newcomers, the experience is like acting out the feelings and thoughts of their teenage years — regardless how old they are chronologically.

A good foundation in the first three Steps is essential for maintaining sobriety during the first few years. As one AA member shared at a meeting: it is like a good building with an excellent foundation. The first three floors must be strong and firm with a strong spiritual quality, and then the rest of the floors, built through years of continuing sobriety, will remain a solid building.

Special Thanks

My 27 years of sobriety were based on a solid foundation because I attended at least four or five meetings a week in the Washington, DC area during the first few years of my sobriety. I also became involved with the 12 Steps, and had an excellent hearing AA sponsor. But all this would not be possible if it were not for several wonderful sign language interpreters who volunteered to interpret at those meetings during the early 70s.

I would like to give thanks to the following interpreters who worked with me during these days: Mary Ann Royster, Rudy Gawlik, Maryann McDermot Cowan, Carol Patrie, Ginny Lewis, Mary Eileen Paul, Joe Rosenstein, Carol Pace, Dennis Cokely, Virginia Covington, and Beverly Walton.

The Growth of this Book

Besides being a professional artist, I have a career working as an addiction counselor and consultant, and have worked with deaf people for the past 20 years. I've developed expertise in areas of addiction, including alcoholism and deafness; Deaf culture; American Sign Language and the signs for drug and alcohol use. I have provided consultation and training to therapists and staff members of treatment programs. I have taught about addiction to both hearing and deaf people, those who work professionally with deaf people, and those who work with sign language interpreters. In this book, the stories and information sharing are based on my experiences with many recovering deaf people, their family members and friends, some of my consumers' cases, and experiences shared by my colleagues.

It is hoped that this book will reach out to as many people as possible, both deaf and hearing, who are involved with the lives of deaf recovering people, and to those who are in recovery themselves.

Chapter One

Challenges: Who Are the Deaf Substance Abusers?

At a conference about deaf people and recovery, participants decided to have "closed 12 Step meetings" nightly — that is, meetings open only to those who are in recovery. The first night, about 35 people attended, almost all of whom were deaf. There were members of AA (Alcoholics Anonymous), ACOA (Adult Children of Alcoholics), NA (Narcotics Anonymous), Al-Anon (family and friends), and others from related 12 Step programs. A hearing AA member who attended this meeting became upset that by mixing different recovery programs in one meeting, this group wasn't following a 12 Traditions guideline. But this was a situation where the need for bonding with other recovering deaf people was stronger than the need to follow rules set up by a majority (hearing) culture — rules that ignore some basic needs of deaf people in a hearing society. This is a case where Deaf culture appropriately took priority over individual differences.

Who are these deaf alcoholics, addicts, co-dependents, and their dysfunctional family members? How are they different from hearing people in the program? What about deaf people who are not involved in Deaf culture or do not use American Sign Language (ASL)? Social service agencies that provide vocational rehabilitation, education and training programs, counseling, and other support services, including Social Security benefits, often fail to properly educate their staff about deaf issues or prepare them for encounters with deaf substance abusers.

Treatment programs which provide deaf services indicate that many of their deaf patients are failing in some important aspect of their lives: they are high school students who have been suspended from school, college drop-outs, unemployed, under-employed, and drunk drivers. They may have been referred to treatment programs by school administrators, employers, family members or by a court order. Many of them have language problems and weak communication abilities in both English and ASL. Signing skills vary; many individuals may use different sign language systems such as signed English, or home signs instead of ASL. Unfortunately, many know and understand little or nothing about Deaf culture.

Before going on to meet these individuals, however, readers should note a couple of conventions used in this book. First is the difference between "deaf" and "Deaf." Adapting a practice proposed by James Woodward (1972), the lowercase "deaf" refers to the audiological condition of not hearing, and the uppercase "Deaf" refers to the particular group of deaf people who identify themselves as a distinct linguistic and cultural minority. For clarity however, we will only use the uppercase "D" when *not* to do so would cause confusion. The terms "Deaf culture" and "Deaf community" are capitalized because of their specific reference to culture — in the same manner as "African-American culture" and "Hispanic community" would be capitalized.

Second, there are some instances where the only proper, clear expression of the thought is through American Sign Language, not written English. In the few places that occur in this book, we have chosen to use the sign-gloss convention of all CAPITAL LETTERS. Those familiar with signs will be able to translate these in their heads, seeing a deaf person's signs and expressions. Readers unfamiliar with signs will still be able to understand the sentences.

Kate's Story

I can't remember the first drink, but I can remember vaguely when I was exposed to drinking. Many of us have that first taste of alcohol when a parent offers a sip from their own drink as a joke. That happened to me. I remember the feeling. I felt superior and proud, probably because my father was the one who offered. I felt good.

My family split up when I was about three years old, around the same time I became deaf from spinal meningitis. My mother had custody of me and my twin sisters who are hearing. My mother found a placement for me at a school that has a deaf program. My mother and a teacher from this school agreed that I would be staying at the teacher's home during the week. Every weekend my mom would come out to get me and take me home. Eventually, that teacher, who already had a family that included her husband and two sons, became my legal guardian because my real mom was not able to follow through on her agreements and take care of me.

Growing up was not easy for me. My real mom is a chronic alcoholic. She was not violent, but she was unable to relate. She was distant and wrapped up in her bottle of booze. When I was 12 and visiting with my mom, she offered the bottle to me. For both of us to deal with each other, it seemed the only way. I drank. This continued every time I visited my mom. I did not understand at the time that it would get me in trouble. My father was not a drinker, but he was not much of a father, either. I don't see much of him. My guardian and her family were good to me, but I was confused about the whole family situation. I think I was just hurt.

My drinking got worse when I went to a residential school for the deaf. I did not know how to socialize unless I was drinking. I thought it was a fun way to get along with kids at school. My drinking led me to using drugs like marijuana and LSD. During my high school days, I would go with a friend on weekends to a big city where I would go to a deaf club. We partied and got very high there. At first, I was doing well in my classes in spite of my drinking and drugging, but as time went on, it got to where I was no longer doing well at school. I managed to graduate, and decided that I would not go to college in the fall. I needed a break because of a very bad experience: I had a bad joint of pot that drove me crazy, and I lost my virginity to a couple of strangers who were much older than me. I was only 16. I became angry and afraid. I continued to drink, but stopped using marijuana.

Although I experienced several more bad situations over the next several years because of my drinking and using, I continued to get high. I became depressed and lonely. It was not until my guardian mom suggested that I get into a treatment program that I realized the seriousness of my problem. She brought me to the program and stayed with me until I finally got admitted. I was 22. It was hard. I did not want to give up my addiction, but I stayed on to complete the program. I stayed there for 49 days. I learned, and finally embraced the fact that I was an addict. I went to AA meetings with an interpreter every day. There were a couple of other deaf patients who came in later. They were admitted by a court order. I could not identify much nor could I communicate well with them because they were different in educational level and culture. One of them could not even sign very well, which sometimes slowed down the group process during our sessions.

After the treatment, I had a hard time starting over without drugs and alcohol. A few times I went to AA meetings in my hometown with an interpreter who was my best friend. It was difficult for me to talk and share at meetings with her interpreting things that I did not even want her to know. We stopped going to these meetings, but I tried to continue attending AA meetings at least once a month at the treatment program, which was about an hour's drive away from my home. I was really unhappy, and I did not feel good about my recovery. I tried to hang in there, but I needed more support. I had a relapse and had to go back to the treatment program. I stayed there for another two weeks, but it was worth it. Afterwards I felt renewed and full of hope. My guardian mom was very patient and supportive. Our relationship has slowly improved, and now we are best friends.

Recently, I moved away from home, and I am now back at college. I am still working on my recovery one day at a time. I have made new friends, deaf and hearing, who are in the program. I go to three interpreted AA meetings a week, which is a huge difference from when I attended only one or two meetings a month during my first year of sobriety back at home. I am still struggling, though, to avoid relapses. It is good having these deaf friends in the program, and I feel much better. I will keep trying to stay clean and sober one day at a time. It is the only way to go for me.

Deaf Persons who have Professional Careers

This does not mean that educated deaf persons of all ages, including these who have professional careers or are currently attending post secondary schools do not have problems with alcohol and drugs. Many of those with professional careers are in treatment under court order, after driving under the influence (DUI) or driving while intoxicated (DWI), to attend 12 Step meetings and counseling sessions. However, they seldom turn up in treatment programs that provide services for deaf patients. They trust no one, including hearing and deaf treatment staff and interpreters, and refuse to identify themselves with the other deaf patients who are "less educated or culturally different." These professional deaf persons are often in strong denial of their problem or they are too ashamed.

Allison

Allison is a young, deaf professional who is new to recovery. She tries to take on the responsibility of setting up a deaf group when she is just 30 days sober, apparently forgetting her own needs for maintenance. Allison has a relapse and realizes she needs help, so she contacts a recovering deaf friend, Dorothy, to help her find a place in a detoxification center. Dorothy gives her a list of treatment programs and indicates the ones that are most willing to provide interpreting services during the treatment. Allison calls the program, but finds out that she cannot begin treatment right away. The admissions staff tells her that she will need to wait a few days so that they can make arrangements to obtain interpreters before she comes in. Dorothy advises her to go home and do the best she can to prepare herself for withdrawal by attending AA/NA meetings over the weekend. Dorothy takes Allison home, loans her just enough money for bus and subway transportation, and gives her enough food to last for a few days until Allison can enter the program.

Allison does not go to interpreted meetings that weekend because she is too embarrassed and angry with another recovering deaf friend, and does not want to see her at these meetings. She knows that it is important for her to attend AA/NA meetings as part of her withdrawal process prior to being admitted to a treatment program. She says she will go to the meetings near her home even though there are no sign language interpreters available. She somehow manages to remain sober on her own until she can begin the program.

The problems described above are commonly faced by deaf people: (1) Even in crisis, they may need to wait for entrance to critical programs because interpreters are not available for immediate admission; and (2) Shame and denial may interfere with accepting help that is available. Allison could not take advantage of the interpreted AA/NA meetings that were available because she was too ashamed to face other recovering deaf friends, or meet new deaf friends. She felt inferior after failing to remain sober on her own.

Allison's story is typical of many deaf and hard of hearing persons who want to recover and start a new alcohol and drug-free life. There are obstacles that they face beginning the recovery process as a result of their previous attitudes, experiences, behaviors and perspectives toward themselves. They must contend with the breakdown of social relationships as well as with the stigma of being deaf in a hearing world. For example, a typical recovering deaf person who has been actively involved in the Deaf community in the past may need to find new friends. Her old drinking and using buddies, who have worked with her on many deaf events, are still in touch with her. Allison realizes that she and her friends are no longer comfortable with each other. Even though they know and respect that she is trying to quit drinking and using, she has to try to avoid them as much as possible because she doesn't feel strong enough to resist the alcohol and drugs that they have.

Old friends who are not in recovery are wary and resistant to her intentions to recover. In the past, they were hurt by Allison's broken promises and bad behavior during her drinking and drugging episodes. Unfortunately, even when she tries to recover, some may never be forgiving. They are weary and burned out from constantly trying to help her. She is trying to take more responsibility for her own actions, but her friends are not sure if these changes are permanent. They do not trust her to maintain her sobriety. This leaves her without her old friends, even though they appreciate that she no longer drinks and causes trouble. They avoid her, waiting to see how long she will remain sober.

If there are some recovering deaf people in the area, she may seek out the meetings they attend and try to form relationships with them. Most of the recovering deaf members are newly sober, and this may create problems, especially if some of them have difficulties staying sober. For example, not long after assisting Allison, Dorothy tried to help Jane with her problems in staying sober and let Jane stay at her home for a few days. But Jane became restless and wanted to use again. She convinced Dorothy to take her to her boyfriend's apartment. Trying to protect Jane, Dorothy accompanied Jane to her boyfriend's place. After they arrived, Jane became violent, demanding heroin and attacking her boyfriend. Dorothy had to leave immediately. Fearful for her own sobriety, Dorothy told Jane that she could not stay with her, and that she was on her own. Fortunately, Dorothy understood that she needed to focus on her own recovery.

There are not many deaf people who are in recovery to become friends with, so Dorothy and Allison may attempt to make friends with hearing AA people, even though most of them are not familiar with sign language and deaf people. Even if a few are willing to learn, it takes a long time for anyone to become fluent in a new language. In the meantime, it is possible to use pencil and paper to write notes back and forth, but even this is not a simple solution. For many deaf people in recovery, English is a second language. They may be unsure of themselves and embarrassed about their inability to write standard English. If they are willing to try, they usually discover that most hearing AA members are not concerned about the rules of English grammar. The basic concepts that the deaf people wish to express about their sobriety issues can be understood even if their sentences are not perfectly composed.

Loneliness and low self-esteem are the two most common factors that lead to relapse. For almost anyone to be successful, the process of recovery requires interaction among AA/NA friends. In fact, recovery can rarely be accomplished without this constant support. It is an essential part of recovery from the disease of alcoholism and drug abuse.

The Disease Concept and Terminology

It is crucial to reexamine the disease concept in order to grasp the challenges recovering people must face. Several terms related to recovery need to be clarified to help readers understand this complex process.

First of all, addiction (alcoholism and substance abuse) is not a choice. It is a disease. Just like cancer, heart disease, and diabetes, it is a chronic illness that produces long term physical, psychological, and social damage. Terence Gorski in his book, *Passages through Recovery,* (1989, pp. 3-9), defines clearly the following terms that are related to disease and recovery:

Chemical dependency (or substance abuse) is a disease that causes a person to lose control over the use of alcohol or other drugs. It is an addiction. This loss of control causes physical, psychological, social, and spiritual problems. The total person is affected.

Abstinence from mood-altering chemicals is the first requirement of recovery. We have to do this before we can learn what to do to get and stay healthy in all areas of our lives. Abstinence is the beginning of sobriety.

Recovery is a developmental process. Addicts don't recover overnight. They pass through a series of stages. The term "developmental" means to grow in stages or steps. It is the gradual effort to learn new and progressively more complex skills. A developmental model of recovery means that we can "grow from simple abstinence to a meaningful and comfortable sobriety."

Sobriety is living without the need for alcohol or other drugs. In recovery, we move from a destructive dependence on alcohol or other drugs toward complete physical, psychological, social and spiritual health. When we stop using chemicals, we begin to heal the damage to our bodies, minds, relationships, and spirit. Sobriety is a way of thinking, a way of acting, a way of relating to others.

With these definitions in mind, this chapter provides background information about deaf substance abusers by explaining some basic reasons for their behavior and perspectives about life.

Deaf Substance Abusers

Deaf people who have alcohol and drug problems come from a wide variety of backgrounds. Most have grown up in hearing families. More than 90% of deaf children are born to hearing parents who have no prior relationship with deaf people. As these deaf children grow up, they often experience loneliness and lack of communication within their own families. More often than not, hearing family members do not learn sign language. Their deaf child is left out during their family discussions and also misses out on much of the casual information hearing people take for granted. Alcohol and drugs can ease or even obliterate feelings of alienation. Sometimes it is not until they are in recovery that deaf adults, sober and with their minds clear, experience culture shock along with the stark realization of how much they were missing because there was little or no communication in their family.

Even when hearing parents or siblings do learn sign language, barriers may still exist. Sometimes a family member will even become involved in some activities in the Deaf community, perhaps as a teacher of deaf children, an interpreter, a counselor, or a strong advocate. The family may seem to have good communication with everyone included on a daily basis. Nevertheless, the deaf member often feels like an outsider and may turn to drugs or alcohol.

Furthermore, a colleague who was a social work student at Gallaudet University did research on deaf patients in a state mental hospital deaf unit a few years ago. He was doing a paper on deaf adult children of alcoholics in this mental institution, and discovered that with two-thirds ($2/3$) of the deaf patients, one or both parents were alcoholics. *In the News,* September 16, 1997, by the American Academy of Otolaryngology-Head and Neck Surgery, indicated that "Children with prenatal alcohol exposures, especially those with fetal alcohol syndrome (FAS), have a high incidence of sensorineural hearing loss (damage to the sensory nerve of hearing) and middle ear disease." This is the conclusion of research completed by Ted Rheney, MD, Will F. McGuirt, Jr., and Tamison Jewett, MD, all from the Bowman Gray School of Medicine in Winston-Salem, NC.

Authors Harlan Lane, Robert Hoffmeister, and Ben Bahan in *A Journey into the Deaf-World,* (p. 161) explain that,

> The anomaly of having culturally different parents is then both a centrifugal and centripetal force in the DEAF-WORLD. It tends to splinter and separate Deaf people in several ways. It discourages their pride in their minority identity. It delays their language acquisition. It may well lead to their education, isolated from other Deaf pupils and role models, in the local hearing school. It frequently

commits them, through articulation drills and cochlear implant surgery, to values and behaviors repellent to members of the DEAF-WORLD. At the same time, the anomaly propels Deaf people toward the DEAF-WORLD, since identification with the DEAF-WORLD offers pride, language, instruction, role models, a culturally compatible spouse, and more that cannot be had elsewhere.

Deaf people who have deaf parents may not have communication problems, but may encounter other obstacles. Deaf addicts who have deaf families tend not to get help with their drug and alcohol problems for a long time. One of the reasons may be that the family members are in denial. They want to avoid shame and deaf gossip in the deaf world and to protect and shelter this addict from the hearing world as well.

Professionals familiar with treatment and deaf people identify a level of substance abuse in the deaf community that is at least equal to the traditional field estimate of 8% to 10% of general population (Grant, et al, 1988).

In his presentation "Empowerment Through Advocacy by Deaf People for Meaningfully Accessible Substance Abuse/Alcoholism Treatment" at the Conference on Substance Abuse and Recovery: Empowerment of Deaf Persons, June 4-5, 1990, Dr. William McCrone stated

> ...there is published evidence that substance abuse and addiction are up to three times more common in the disability community than in the general population (Gorski, 1980; Steitler, 1984, Greer, Roberts & Jenkins, 1990) ...Many people with disabilities have overwhelming additional burdens in life that may be relieved by alcohol and drug abuse, or "self-medication." Deaf children and other children with disabilities are frequently overmedicated or inappropriately medicated (Cohen, 1979) for behavioral problems that can result when there is inadequate communication at home and at school. (p. 105-106)

Dr. McCrone (1994) projects that there are approximately 5,105 deaf crack users; 3,505 deaf heroin users; 31,915 deaf cocaine users; and 97,745 deaf marijuana users in the U.S. today.

Education

Educational programs for deaf students vary in attitude and approach. As adults, deaf people often define themselves by their educational experience. Until recently, most deaf students attended residential deaf schools, either programs that allowed sign language or oral schools where signing was forbidden and the emphasis was on speech and lipreading. Most parents today prefer day schools, especially mainstream programs in public schools. Mainstream programs for deaf students may provide notetakers, interpreters, and deaf-only classes during all or part of the school day. Students may also attend regular classes, usually with an interpreter, during part of the day. Since deaf people make up such a small percentage of the population, it is rare that there are enough deaf students to make a critical mass in the local community. Even in the best mainstream programs, deaf students miss out on a lot of socialization experience and can never take communication for granted.

Deaf Adults Who are Educationally Retarded

There are many deaf adults who are educationally retarded for various reasons. They appear to be limited in knowing American Sign Language and English. This is probably due to physical or organic brain problems that occur from birth, illness, or accidents that cause brain injury. There are several types of people that may require different educational approaches for them to understand the basic problems of using and drinking. These may include deaf individuals with low functioning abilities (they are sometimes labeled as ones with minimal language), or ones with insufficient education (for example, some families keep their deaf children home, away from educational facilities). There are some deaf individuals who are mentally retarded due to illness or as a birth defect. Regular AA/NA meetings may not be effective for these types of deaf people who may not even understand ASL sign language interpreters. Also, to place them at an all-deaf meeting with other deaf people in recovery who are more educated would not be effective, either. Educational meetings geared to these different types of people, provided by professionals or specialists in working with this population, may more be effective.

Growing Up Dependent

Significantly, one of the few things that all early educational programs for deaf students have in common is that they are controlled mainly by hearing adults. In fact, many deaf people do not meet any deaf adults until they grow up themselves. During infancy or early childhood, most are given hearing tests and other related evaluations by medical professionals such as ear, nose, and throat doctors or audiologists, who are trained in diagnosis, not language or culture. The children and their parents are referred to education programs also staffed by hearing people who have little knowledge themselves about what it means to grow up as a deaf person.

For many deaf children, communication difficulties lead to little or no power to influence decisions, and this continues far longer for them than for their hearing counterparts. Deaf children feel powerless long past the point when hearing children normally start to learn to make decisions for themselves and to accept the consequences.

For recovering deaf people, the ramifications of growing up learning to be dependent and powerless are especially crucial. They are overly dependent on hearing people or other deaf people who have been in recovery for a long time. They are reluctant to take full responsibility for themselves. Yet, part of the learning process in recovery involves learning to practice responsibility by assuming simple tasks like making coffee at AA meetings, or becoming the program secretary or treasurer for the meetings. It can be a new concept to deaf people that for them to grow, they need to take what they learn and pass it on to others. The concept of service to others can be quite foreign to those who have grown up dependent, especially upon hearing people, and have learned to take, but not to give or share.

The Impact of Being Deaf

The impact of being deaf or hard of hearing can be very different depending on circumstances. Individuals who are born deaf or hard of hearing, or who lose their hearing at an early age, have a very different kind of experience than people who become deaf later in life. Deaf children may pick up negative feelings about their lack of hearing from their parents, from their siblings or from other children, but in general, they regard themselves as complete. On the other hand, deafened adults have a deep sense of loss. They have more of a stake in preserving life as they have known it. Many newly deafened adults suffer from denial, shown by such things as not informing others that they have some hearing loss, refusing to use hearing aids, and not learning to use TTYs and or other adaptive equipment such as closed captioning devices for their television sets. For some people, the impact of loss outweighs the benefits of acceptance, even when they "know" better.

For example, Rosie was a sign language interpreter whose elderly parents were both losing their hearing. In their denial, they refused to learn sign language from their daughter. Rosie signed and talked simultaneously with them despite their objections. As time went by, Rosie stopped using her voice. Her parents are now reading her signs without realizing or acknowledging it. Nevertheless, they do not identify themselves as deaf persons.

Deafened

The term "deafened" is used for people whose onset of deafness came later in life, from accident, illness, or certain drugs. Most communicate in a variety of ways, including speechreading, signs, and real-time captioning. Because they became deaf later in life, only a few use or depend on sign language, and those who do most often communicate not in signs taken from ASL but those arranged in English word order.

In "On Signing with a Hearing Accent" by Laurel E. Glass and Holly H. Elliot, in *Deaf American Monograph: Deafness: Life and Culture,* (1994), the authors attempted to help clarify what these deafened adults are experiencing:

> When a hearing person "becomes deaf" or "becomes hard of hearing" they continue to "think hearing"... A Deaf person may understand best when they consider a hearing person who loses hearing is the same as a Deaf person losing vision. Think what the loss of sign language would mean for communication and to relationships. Consider the enormous cost — in time, in thought, in energy — of learning new skills to cope as a Deaf person who no longer sees ASL. Hearing loss is LOSS. It is tough to deal with.
>
> ...Deaf really are different from deaf in life experience, in language, in skills, in the knowledge and resources needed to deal with no or little sound.
>
> ...When a deafened person does not learn ASL, or signs awkwardly in English word order, or signs and talks at the same time, it is not a rejection of deafness. It is an attempt to do the best they can to adapt to a change in their lives for which they have little training and less knowledge. More than that, for many who become deaf or hard of hearing, the hearing loss focuses changes in life style, changes in relationships with others, changes in awareness of themselves, often changes in how they earn a living.
>
> ...Initially, at least, the changes from hearing to not hearing are often so large that they can properly be called "disabling." Although adaptation finally may occur, accomplishing it is rarely easy or a complete success.

Betty G. Miller

Some deafened adults do eventually become part of the Deaf community, working with and living with other deaf people, but many do not. I. King Jordan, Gallaudet University's first deaf president, is a deafened adult who lost his hearing because of a motorcycle accident at the age of 21. He later became a student at Gallaudet, and entered the Deaf community. However, many deafened adults are uncomfortable being grouped with culturally Deaf people.

The initial sense of loss and the accompanying grief have a huge impact on the deafened person's life. This grief is felt not only as loss of hearing but also as a loss of career and status. Many deafened adults are already secure in their career or professional life, working as teachers, doctors, CPAs, graphic artists, veterinarians, and various other occupations. Sometimes because of the age of onset of deafness or because their work doesn't require much interaction with people, deafened adults may continue in their job. Other late deafened adults may continue their careers but incorporate a Deaf life into their work. A hearing teacher who loses her hearing, for example, might later decide to work with deaf students.

But the primary difference between Deaf people and those who become deafened is the focus on loss, especially the loss of easy interaction within the culture in which they were raised. Deafened patients who are in recovery may find themselves with serious identity problems. They may be confused in relating to others, both deaf and hearing. Those who enter the Deaf community are experiencing a tremendous change — one that affects their whole life in every aspect. They are challenged by questions of their identity, of their tolerance and/or acceptance of Deaf norms, as well as by learning how to deal with a world that has suddenly become totally visual.

A deafened individual's sense of loss requires that they find some means of adapting to that loss. They may deny their own deafness and refuse to adapt to the situation, especially during their drinking and using days. The treatment program staff of the deaf unit may also face some serious difficulties in communicating with them, especially with those patients who have no sign language skills. The deafened patients may not have enough lipreading and/or speech training or other skills to even try to communicate with their counselors.

Culturally Deaf People

Most Deaf people who were born deaf into Deaf families do not have the same sense of loss connected with their deafness. Instead, the focus is on shared cultural norms and values with others in the Deaf community. Most Deaf parents these days are delighted to find they have a Deaf baby. These Deaf children begin signing at an early age, similar to the language acquisition process of hearing children when they are exposed to spoken language. In Deaf homes, the preferred language is ASL, and devices such as TTYs, flashing signal lights for the doorbell and telephone, and captioned TV are as normal as stereos and door chimes are to hearing families. Sound and speech have little or no importance to them.

Some of those with hearing families who go to deaf schools become culturally Deaf. They develop and share cultural norms and values at the school. They may be reluctant to go home during school breaks, and prefer to be or remain at school, not at their homes, especially if there is little or no communication access with their families.

Hard of Hearing

The term "hard of hearing" generally refers to a person with a mild to moderate hearing loss. Sometimes a hard of hearing person will "hear" fairly well, but not be able to discriminate speech. Often hard of hearing people can benefit from technology that amplifies or clarifies sound such as hearing aids, phone amplifiers, audio-loop systems, and digital and audio systems. Many hard of hearing people do not learn sign language or become part of the Deaf community. Others do, identifying themselves as Deaf and associating with Deaf people, despite the fact they are audiologically hard of hearing. Often they are not accepted by Deaf people regardless of how little they actually can hear. These hard of hearing individuals are truly between two worlds and are often rejected by both the Deaf world and the hearing world. This dilemma creates confusion with personal identity and hinders the process of recovery for these hard of hearing persons beginning their quest for sobriety.

There are many levels and degrees of hearing loss that can determine a person's identity and his or her place in society, both in the hearing world and the Deaf world. There are differences in experience even within the hard of hearing community. There is a significant difference between children who grow up hard of hearing and adults who become hard of hearing later in life. Hard of hearing children are generally "mainstreamed" in hearing schools, sometimes with special programs and support services, often not. Those who gradually lose their hearing later in life, either because of aging or because of injury or disease, have grown up as hearing people. Their feelings of loss are often the same as deafened people because they are experiencing a shutting-out of the life that is familiar to them.

Brynn's Story

I grew up hard of hearing. For me this meant that I was expected to be a hearing person who couldn't hear very well. Hearing aids, weekly speech lessons, and regular visits to the audiologist and "ear doctor" were the only formal concessions to my "hearing loss" during my childhood. I was good at this, learning to talk and lipread to the extent that most people meeting me didn't know right away that I couldn't hear them well. I never knew anyone else in my entire life while growing up who was deaf or hard of hearing. I knew there had to be others, because the words existed, but I never met them.

School was hard. There were no notetakers back then, and no concept of mainstreaming and support services for hard of hearing children. The fact that I was smarter than most of the children in my classes was the biggest reason I survived my schooling and got a good education. Everything succeeds with smart children, which is why we're usually picked to be the examples of the success of whatever educational method we were subjected to — regardless of the actual value of the method.

Hardest were the courses that required class participation. I learned to stop volunteering to answer questions from the teacher because of the ridicule or shame that came when I said the same thing another student had just said — as if I was stupid for not hearing that first answer instead of being credited for thinking of the answer myself.

By the time I was in high school, my dad's drinking was getting to me. It was hurting the entire family, and I talked with some of my friends about this problem. I even found out about Ala-Teen, the AA program for teenagers who have alcoholic parents. But I didn't get any help.

Why? Because of what I now recognize as internalized oppression. When I found out about Ala-Teen, I immediately rejected it as an option simply because it meant going to group meetings. While I functioned just fine one-on-one with hearing people, groups were torture. By the time I had figured out who was talking, they were done and I had missed it all.

It wasn't until I was in my mid-twenties that I discovered deaf people, learned ASL, began using interpreters and entered the deaf community. It wasn't until my early thirties that I finally got help with my dad's drinking, by learning about ACOAs (Adult Children of Alcoholics) and going to their meetings — interpreted meetings, deaf meetings, and a deaf counselor changed my life forever, for which I'm eternally grateful.

If hard of hearing persons have sign language skills, they will more likely use sign language interpreters in their support group meetings. Those who do not know signs, but who have the ability to speechread, may attend small AA speakers meetings where they can focus on one speaker, sometimes using an audio loop for amplification. They have the right to oral interpreters, but often do not know such interpreters exist, do not have speechreading skills, or are too ashamed or too reluctant to appear "different" that they won't use them.

Generally, AA group meetings are difficult for deafened and hard of hearing people to follow. By the time they have identified who is talking, that person has often stopped and another person has begun speaking. By the time they catch up with the new speaker, they have missed the beginning of the story, so the remainder doesn't make much sense. Hard of hearing adults are often accused of hearing only what they want to hear. This attitude can cause the treatment counselor to misjudge the deafened or hard of hearing clients' motives. The counselor may believe the client is resisting counseling, when in fact she has not heard all the information correctly.

One way that an AA group can support a hard of hearing or deafened person who does not know sign language is for the members to slow down and identify themselves by raising their hands before they start speaking. This will usually only happen in small groups of about four or five people where everyone is committed to a process of inclusion and the group dynamics are agreed upon in advance and maintained.

Dr. McCay Vernon and Randy Inskip in their book, *The Randy Inskip Story* explained that:

> ...hard of hearing people are the least understood of any group in our society. People cannot "see" the disability. It is invisible. Because it is unseen, the public does not understand it. Instead of a sensitivity to hearing loss, the public is aware only of the trouble and frustration they have in communicating with a person who does not always respond. Even when there is a response, it is sometimes incorrect.
>
> All hard of hearing people have had the experience of people being impatient with them ... This may be coupled with the "funny" speech often associated with hearing loss

… The public often thinks that the hard of hearing person is not too bright, and in general, not very capable.

Randy, like many hard of hearing people, usually felt reasonably comfortable in talking to people only one to one.

Group situations are much more complex and difficult. Randy could never follow the interactive communication that goes on in a hearing group discussion because hard of hearing people are unable to detect the direction sounds are coming from. In a group discussion, he was not able to identify the speaker and then would get lost in the dynamics of the different conversations that may be going on almost simultaneously.

Like Randy, some hard of hearing people do identify themselves as Deaf and choose to associate with culturally Deaf people, despite the fact that they are audiologically hard of hearing. Cultural anthropologists seem to agree that hard of hearing people suffer most with issues of identity. They are not "hearing" people and their hearing friends often find it hard to integrate the hard of hearing person into the hearing household. They are not "Deaf" because the Deaf community often will reject non signers regardless of how little they hear. Even when hard of hearing people are fluent in ASL, there is a subtle resentment among Deaf people. Some may be envious, but most often they are ambivalent about the value of someone's abilities to use voice phones or to communicate verbally with hearing people. In some situations, they may find themselves dependent on hard of hearing friends. Yet, in the Deaf world, these skills are not necessary. This leaves hard of hearing people caught between two worlds, and often makes them feel rejected by both, leading to confusion and despair.

Allen's Story

Allen is a hard of hearing man who was ordered by the court to either enter a one year drug treatment program or be incarcerated for two years. Allen and his public aid lawyer agreed to admission to a treatment program. Unfortunately, the court refused to be responsible for follow-up and to see that a sign language interpreter was provided for Allen in his individual and group sessions and meetings. Allen had no choice but enter this treatment program. He tried to make do with speechreading, writing notes back and forth, and gestures. One time, an interpreter was provided when there was training on ASL and Deaf culture. Allen took advantage of the interpreter's presence to express his concerns and feelings to a group of other patients and staff members regarding communication. However, Allen completed his program before anything could be done about improving accessibility. It appeared that he benefited very little from the program because a few weeks later, he had a relapse.

When hard of hearing AA members have sign language skills, they usually prefer to use interpreters in the AA meetings. They will probably use their own speech instead of using sign language and letting the interpreter voice for them. This may be a problem. If a hard of hearing person's voice is unclear, members must speak up and ask the person to use the interpreter to voice. An option for hard of hearing members who do not know sign language is to go to a "speakers" meeting, where there are always at least two speakers sharing their experiences to a group of AA members. The hard of hearing person can easily lipread the speakers by focusing on one person talking at a time. Amplification devices may also improve communication.

Putting All Recovering Deaf People in One Program

Is it a good idea to place all kinds of deaf people in one treatment program deaf unit? Here are two stories to consider that bring out some questions about placing all deaf people in the same program. The first story describes how one deaf person may influence and limit the progress of other deaf persons in a recovery program. The second shows how the past can catch up with a person too early in their recovery.

Terry, Wilbur, and Joe

Three deaf patients are admitted to a treatment program. They are Terry, Wilbur, and Joe, and they come from different family and educational backgrounds, although they are all African-American. Terry, who is in denial about his addiction, is very negative, self-centered. He constantly belittles the other two deaf patients, Wilbur and Joe, by remarking on their weak signing skills and poor English, making them feel low and uncomfortable.

Terry has grown up in a school for the deaf, and he is aggressive and arrogant. He started using marijuana and was suspended from school several times. After he left school, his addictive behaviors worsened and he began using other drugs, including crack.

Wilbur and Joe attended different schools. Wilbur had an all-deaf class once a week, and attended other classes with a sign language interpreter. Joe attended all hearing classes with a sign language interpreter. The sign language interpreters used signed English and did not have ASL skills. Both Wilbur and Joe had very limited interaction with the hearing students, and there were only one or two other students in their schools who were deaf. Wilbur and Joe's sign language skills are mixed. They often use signs in English word order, and their understanding of both English and ASL is limited. Their parents and siblings were hearing and did not use sign language. Neither Wilbur or Joe had appropriate opportunities to develop social skills with other people, deaf or hearing.

During their stay at the treatment program, Terry would relentlessly badger Wilbur and Joe, insulting these deaf men who already had low self-esteem. Nevertheless, they would not report Terry to the hearing counselors in the treatment program. They had obviously internalized the cultural norm to be protective of other deaf people regardless of behavior.

Then, after one week's stay, Terry walked out of the treatment program. Over the next few weeks, Wilbur and Joe gradually changed their negative attitudes and became more positive about themselves.

They showed a willingness to change their isolating behaviors and developed some interaction with other patients in the program. They remained in the program until completion, and looked forward to maintaining their sobriety during aftercare. In this case, it seems that Terry's presence, although he is deaf, was a serious barrier to Wilbur and Joe's progress in the early stages of treatment.

Jack

In another instance, Jack, who is deaf and a well known person in the deaf community of the small city where he has lived all his life, decided to stop using drugs. He was a crack addict and both a dealer and buyer of drugs. In the past, he was dealing mostly to his deaf friends.

At first he tried to attend an all-deaf AA/NA meeting, but he discovered that he knew most of the other members of the group. There were already resentments between Jack and some of the other deaf members. Jack, being newly sober, felt uncomfortable being around some of his old friends in the group. Some of them owed him money, and likewise, there were some to whom he owed money. He was not ready to face or cope with the problems he had with them.

Jack's addiction counselor recommended that he attend a hearing daytime recovery program, which provided sign language interpreters, during this early phase of recovery. Jack was encouraged to have individual counseling at least twice a week with his addiction counselor. This was an alternative to confronting his old deaf friends who are in the program. Jack felt safer and more comfortable on his own with professional support for at least a few months.

Situations like these do occur for many deaf individuals who are trying to achieve sobriety. Furthermore, many treatment programs with deaf units bring together all types of deaf people, including signers, non-signers, deafened people, hard of hearing, as well as deaf and hard of hearing people with ethnic and cultural differences. When the non-signers and signers get together, the dynamics of a group process may be slowed down, because they will have to repeat some of the things that have been shared. The deafened adults may not accept their deafness. The Deaf members may feel uncomfortable with them because they have not been accustomed to associating with hearing and deafened adults prior to being in the treatment program. A Deaf patient may have had the experience of being oppressed by hearing people in the past and sees the deafened patient as similar to hearing people. In addition, just as in hearing groups, deaf patients may harbor racist beliefs and misconceptions or stereotyped concepts about individuals from other cultures or ethnic groups.

The main reason for admitting Deaf, deaf, hard of hearing and deafened patients together to deaf units without regard for their diverse backgrounds is because the deaf population is so small. The programs are usually financed by grants or federal funding and require a certain number of participants to justify maintaining the unit. If there are not enough deaf patients requiring these services to fill the quota, the program is in danger of losing its funding. The program staff needs to be especially sensitive to the problems and underlying issues raised by diversity in culture, ethnic background, and deafness.

One solution may be to extend the treatment program. Instead of limiting treatment to 28 to 30 days, six months or even a full year may be more effective, giving patients time to become comfortable with one another and to develop understanding and trust. They need more time to understand their addiction as a disease and to appreciate the importance of support for maintaining sobriety. They must also learn how to advocate for communication access and have the time to explore underlying issues in order to understand the impact of Deaf culture and American Sign Language on recovery.

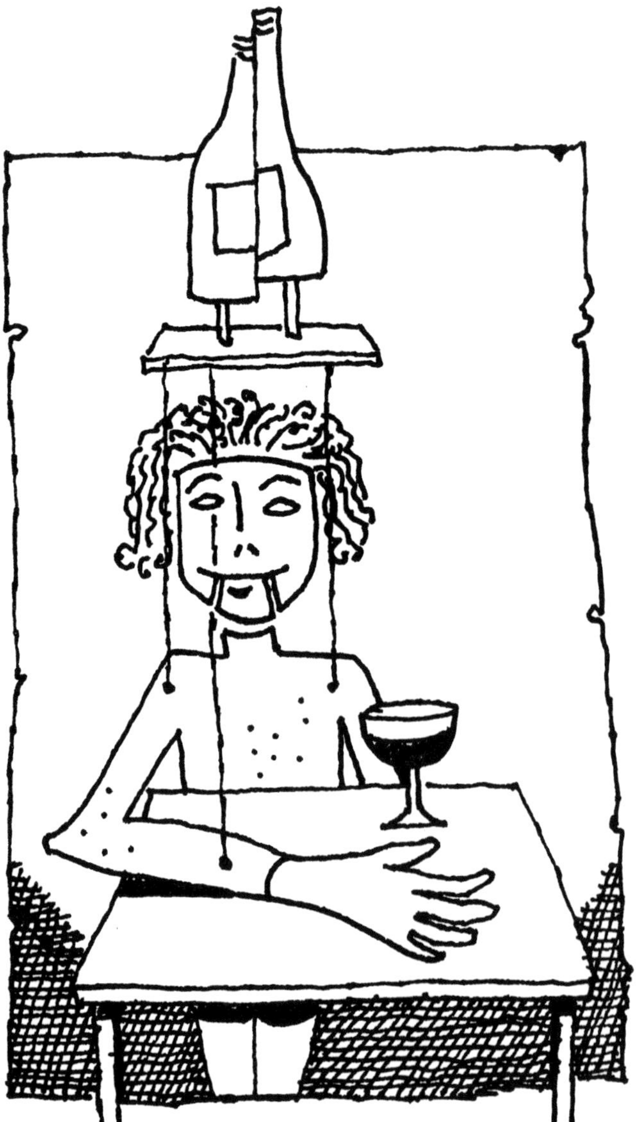

Chapter Two

The Deaf Community, ASL, and Deaf Culture: Impact on Recovering Deaf People

Elizabeth's Story

This is my story. I am a recovering Deaf alcoholic and drug addict. I want to share my experience, strength, and hope. I am doing this to help myself. I need to stay sober. After completing a 28-day inpatient program, I went home thinking and wondering what I must do to stay sober. I know that I need to attend AA/NA meetings, find an AA/NA sponsor, and continue visits with an addiction counselor. I cannot be with my old friends who still use and drink heavily. I must try to find new friends.

I live in a small community where there are not many Deafies. The hearing members of AA/NA groups in this small town must get used to having a Deaf person and a sign language interpreter in their meetings. I need to explain again and again why the interpreter is needed. I try to be part of their group, but communication with them is difficult.

I have to change friends, and try find to new friends. I stop going to Deaf clubs, Deaf bowling events, and Deaf gatherings. Those are the places are where I used to drink and use too much. But I am lonely and do not know where to go. It is a great loss to me, not to be with the Deaf people who are important to me and my Deaf culture. I am disappointed to say that at this important time my Deaf friends do not really understand what I am going through. There are very few Deaf people who are in recovery. I feel rejected and lonely. I need support from Deaf people and the Deaf community, because the Deaf world will always be part of my life.

The Deaf Community

In the larger deaf community, deaf people use many different labels to describe themselves They may identify as "hearing impaired," "hard of hearing," "late deafened," "oral deaf," or "culturally Deaf," based on personal childhood experiences in education, family life, culture, and lifestyle. A small number of hearing people, generally family, friends, interpreters or professionals in related fields, may also consider themselves part of the deaf community. However, Deaf people, who are the main focus of this book, do not think of themselves as disabled, nor as hearing impaired, which implies that the ears are broken. Rather they view themselves as members of a distinct linguistic and cultural minority. They are members of the Deaf community.

The Deaf community is relatively small, close, and has high expectations of conformity from its members. After work, many deaf people socialize only within this community, taking part in events that are deaf-only. Some of the most popular activities of deaf people involve sports, such as bowling, volleyball, or skiing, and other activities that can be done in groups, such as getting together for picnics. Deaf culture has evolved from this segment of the deaf community that shares a language — American Sign Language (ASL) — and from common experiences, values and lifestyles. Until recently, most deaf people attended schools for the deaf, often developing lifelong friendships with classmates. Also, it used to be that the most important community institution was the Deaf Club, which would organize group activities, including sponsoring teams and entering them in deaf regional, national, and international tournaments. Deaf people maintain contact with each other through these tournaments and at the annual or biannual conventions of deaf organizations. However, new technology such as captioned television, computer email, TTYs, and other new devices, as well as various other activities, may have changed all this.

Before the widespread use of TTYs (Teletypewriters, also known as Telecommunication Devices for the Deaf [TDD] or Text Telephones [TT]) in the mid-sixties and early seventies, Deaf people kept abreast of deaf community news by participating in these activities and through the news and gossip carried by deaf printers who travelled all over USA for their jobs. Today, expanded TTY use in the deaf community, along with electronic mail, faxes, and text pagers, news and rumors can travel across the country, and sometimes overseas, much faster than ever before.

Deaf people still carry on the tradition of spreading the news to friends who live far away. For example, Ann was badly bitten by her cat in Washington, DC, and was advised to keep her right arm in a sling for two weeks. Not only did her family members hear about it from other family members, but deaf friends in California learned about it through TTY conversations and email messages. This piece of information is important to deaf people. Her friends were worried because the temporary loss of the use of her arm interfered with Ann's ability to communicate in sign language. Deaf people were concerned that the injury might be permanent and that Ann would not be able to sign well again.

Deaf identity, with its focus on language, values, and lifestyle, can be very complex. Donald, who is profoundly deaf, may consider himself hard of hearing because he grew up in a mainstreamed hearing setting where Deaf culture and ASL did not exist. On the other hand, Anita, who is audiologically hard of hearing, has grown up in a deaf family using American Sign Language and identifies herself as Deaf. A proud young African-American deaf woman, Rosalyn, is concerned about the issues of being Black and Deaf. These differences may become crucial identity issues among recovering deaf people. They ask themselves: Where do I fit into the community? What about the hearing world? The Deaf world? What is Deaf culture? Deafness? Hard of hearing? Who am I?

Betty G. Miller

American Sign Language

American Sign Language (ASL) is a crucial part of Deaf culture and identity in the United States and Canada. It is a complete language with its own syntax and grammar, totally independent from English. Instead of vowels, consonants and syllables, the building blocks of this visual-gestural language are specific movements of the body, head, face, eyes, and hands. Often people are surprised to learn that sign language, like spoken language, is not universal. In fact, because of certain historical events, ASL is very unlike British Sign Language (BSL) but closely related to French Sign Language (Language de France des Sourdes, or LSF).

Signed languages have been formally studied only in the past forty years. Before that, many linguists, as well as most lay people, regarded voice and speech as essential elements of language. However, contemporary research has proven that sign languages can be as complex and elegant as any spoken language. Several countries, particularly those in Scandinavia, have acknowledged the separate and equal status of both signed and spoken national languages.

ASL was recognized as a language by linguists in the early 1970s and the implications of that revelation are still being debated in academic meetings and deaf clubrooms. Although ASL is the preferred language of the Deaf community, its use is still relatively rare in educational settings or programs for deaf children. Few deaf people have the opportunity to actually study the language in the same way that hearing people study English. The growing number of ASL classes are mostly for hearing people interested in learning signs. Advanced classes are usually geared to interpreters or other professionals. Traditionally the language has been passed down from generation to generation within deaf families and from deaf peer to deaf peer at schools for the deaf.

Dr. Clayton Valli, a scholar and ASL poet, has explored the external and internal oppression of deaf people and exposed how some individuals participate in their own oppression by allowing hearing people (or audists) to control and authorize views of deaf people:

> Since 1960, researchers have shown that American Sign Language (ASL) is the natural language for deaf people and that deaf people have their own culture. However, audism and xenophobia still prevent deaf people from being themselves. (An audist makes decisions about everything for deaf people in an effort to "melt" them into "normal" society.) Many audized deaf people have delusions about their true identity. Most are passive, letting audists run their lives.
>
> ...Today very few deaf people have awareness of ASL and of self and are empowered. ...In order to free themselves from being stuck with audists, deaf people must start with their own oppression, the deficiencies of their group. ...Today within the deaf community there are many possibilities to start empowering audized deaf people, including their own languages (ASL and English) and deaf culture.
>
> ("American Sign Language Poetry's Struggle for Existence" by Dr. Clayton Valli, *The Network*, v. 12, p. 45 - 46, Spring, 1996, The Union Institute, Cincinnati, OH.)

Deaf language and cultural studies are still in the early stages. Currently, some deaf leaders with their hearing allies are attempting to win recognition for ASL in the Office of Bilingual Education and Minority Language Affairs (OBEMLA) at the U.S. Department of Education and asking that OBEMLA mandate that ASL be used in bilingual deaf educational programs in the United States. However, many programs and service agencies working with deaf clients have not yet accepted ASL as a language or attempted to educate themselves about Deaf culture.

Betty G. Miller

Perspectives on Culture and Deaf Culture

What is culture? There are actually 300 definitions of "culture" according to Kroeber and Kluckhohn in their book *Culture: a Critical Review of Concepts and Definitions.* "A set of learned behaviors of a group of people" is one general definition of culture. For example, waving a white flag or handkerchief is a universal symbol of surrender. By contrast, using gestures and being belligerent in bargaining is acceptable behavior in an Italian market, but not in an American supermarket. Different groups assign different meanings to colors. In some cultures, people wear white to indicate mourning; in others, black is appropriate.

Deaf Culture

Deaf culture is the term for behaviors that make Deaf people different from others and unite them in a shared world view. Remember Ann and her cat from the beginning of this chapter? The news about Ann and her wounded arm travelled from one deaf person to another across time and space because it is important in the Deaf community. Such information is rarely printed in newspapers such as *Silent News* and *DeafNation,* and of course, never shows up in regular newspapers or on TV. This "grapevine" is an important factor in the development and maintenance of the bond between Deaf people, the bond that creates the Deaf culture.

Views on Deaf Culture

In her research, Dr. Barbara Kannapell examined several different features of culture in the context of the Deaf community. The following examples are from her paper "Recovering Deaf Persons, Identity Issues and the Deaf Culture Impact," *The Next Step Conference Proceedings,* July 5-8, 1992.

- A set of learned behaviors of a group of people: As a social group, deaf people learn how to behave as Deaf.
- A world view shaped by experience: Deaf people develop perceptions about the world and attitudes toward

themselves as Deaf individuals. They also develop attitudes and perceptions of how they see other deaf and hearing people.

- A system sustained and communicated by symbols: American Sign Language is a powerful symbol of Deaf culture.

In addition, Dr. Kannapell also proposed her own definition of Deaf culture and described five significant indicators:

Deaf culture consists of a set of learned behaviors and perceptions that shape the values and norms of Deaf people based on their shared or common experiences. The five basic concepts of Deaf culture are:

1) Communication — because of the absence of hearing, Deaf people use eyes and hands to communicate.
2) Language — a shared language which, in America, is called American Sign Language (ASL).
3) Perceptions — sharing the experience of being deaf shapes values, rules of behavior, and common knowledge.
4) Community — creating a community of Deaf people — by developing a special bond:
    – developing a sense of belonging
    – developing their own identity as deaf persons
    – developing high self-esteem or positive self-image through institutions such as Deaf clubs, Deaf schools, and Deaf organizations.
5) History — sharing stories, jokes, and historical information through Deaf folklore and literature.

Another citation may help clarify the contrast between the medical or audiological perspective and a cultural perspective of Deaf people. Dr. Carol Padden and Dr. Tom Humphries in their book, *Deaf in America, Voices from a Culture*, (p. 24-25), state:

By definition, cultures are highly specific systems that both explain things and constrain how things can be known. Sam (from a Deaf family) wondered why the hearing girl next door behaved so strangely. His mother explained that the girl had some significantly different feature that led her to behave unlike us. Sam found this explanation completely sensible. Howard [also from a Deaf family] never knew he was "deaf" until he started school [a residential deaf school]; his family life did not prepare him for the odd definitions of "deaf" he would later encounter. His is not a story about failing to understand the meaning of deafness, but a story of cultural difference.

...as children living in the world of their caretakers, they are powerfully guided by the conventions of their culture. ...From the stories mentioned above, we see different ways the "recipes" and "instructions" of their worlds guide the perceptions and theories of children like Sam and Howard.

These deaf authors, Dr. Kannapell, Dr. Padden and Dr. Humphries, have written extensively and presented widely about the linguistic and cultural identity of Deaf people. We will not go further into this here, but rather stress that cultural understanding is an important consideration for all professionals who work with recovering deaf people.

David

David, a recovering deaf alcoholic, became sober after 20 years of drinking and started to attend AA meetings. He attended at least four interpreted AA meetings regularly each week with other deaf members. He also attended a weekly deaf group meeting (with deaf and hearing members). The deaf group had volunteer interpreters at its meetings.

Though he was a fluent signer, David considered himself hard of hearing because he was able to use the voice phone and to communicate with hearing people without an interpreter in one-to-one situations. Prior to being in the Alcoholics Anonymous program, he was very active in the Deaf community and almost never associated with hearing people. In fact, he did not have any hearing friends at the time he entered the program. At the same time, he did not appreciate or understand Deaf culture, nor did he feel comfortable with his deaf friends unless he was in a superior position. David's recovery was threatened because he could not relate well with others. He was unable to accept his "deafness" and felt that the other deaf members were inferior to him. He willingly offered support, but if he needed help, emotionally or spiritually, he turned to hearing AA members. He felt that hearing people knew more than deaf people, although he also believed that hearing people would eventually try to take advantage of him or let him down.

David was ambivalent about the deaf and hearing worlds, not recognizing or understanding the cultural differences that were affecting him and other recovering deaf people. He was not aware of the deep, angry feelings he had within himself about Deaf culture, ASL and the hearing world. It may take several years before he begins to clearly understand himself and his identity as a Deaf person. He will have to clarify and resolve these issues about his relationship with himself and other people through counseling and working on his 12 Step program.

Cultural Confusion/Identity Confusion

Like David, many d/Deaf people are confused about their identities. For example, the following statements are based on anecdotes that d/Deaf students at Gallaudet University shared with Dr. Kannapell for her study, *The Role of Deaf Identity in Deaf Studies* (1993):

1) They are told that they are not deaf;
2) They are different from other deaf students;
3) They are almost like hearing people;
4) They are hard of hearing or hearing impaired;
5) They believed that when they grew up, they would become hearing; and

6) They believed that they would die young because they never saw adult Deaf role models.

In her dissertation, *Language Choice – Identity Choice,* Dr. Kannapell stated that:

> Deaf people have a culture and a language (American Sign Language) of their own. Deaf people are bilingual in ASL and English in varying degrees, though some are either ASL or English monolingual. They identify with Deaf culture, both cultures, the hearing culture, or neither. Their attitudes toward the languages and the cultures involved depend largely on several sociolinguistic factors: the functions of the use of the languages, language choice, group reference, and cultural identity. Clearly, in America, the system forces Deaf people to choose one language or culture over the other. Deaf people may feel ambivalent toward the competing languages and cultures. (1993, p. 31.)

Here is a scene that was overheard (overseen) at a Washington, DC bus stop. A similar conversation could take place anywhere deaf youth are gathered and talking about their lives. As they introduce each other and start signing, some are using fluent ASL but others sign awkwardly or in English word order. Nancy asks Joe, "Are you from Gallaudet?" Joe responds: "No, not now. I left Gallaudet University because I felt that Gallaudet has nothing to offer to benefit me. I felt that going to a hearing university will be much better for me. Gallaudet is like a high school to me." Jane says: "I agree with you, but Gallaudet is all right. I really don't know what I want to do. I think I will major in English, but I don't like English." This example indicates the confusion and conflict about identity that affects many deaf people, because Joe is using Gallaudet, a university for deaf students, symbolically. By saying Gallaudet is "like a high school," he is saying that the deaf world is "lagging behind" the hearing world, and he doesn't belong there. This confusion may negatively impact their recovery.

Language, Personal, and Social Identities

Dr. Kannapell also described three major aspects of identity that are strongly interrelated:

> Language identity refers to the language in which a person is most at home. There are three types of language identity among Deaf people: ASL, ASL/English, and English. …It seems clear that Deaf people can have ASL or English in their language identity. …Many Deaf people feel strongly identified with other Deaf people through use of American Sign Language. ASL is a crucial requirement for membership in the community. …However, many Deaf people are ambivalent toward ASL and English as their language identity. …Some of them believe if they used a mixture of ASL and English, they are better off than those who use ASL. They learned from observing teachers who approved of them when they use a mixture of ASL/English.
>
> Most of them use English-like signing with hearing people…there are three possible explanations: 1.) Deaf people are conditioned to use English with hearing people. 2.) Deaf people unconsciously try to please hearing people by meeting their needs and dealing with them on their terms. 3.) Deaf people have low expectations of ASL skills of hearing people. …A Deaf person may be clear, ambiguous, or ambivalent about her language identity.
>
> Personal identity or self identity is how deaf people see themselves… "hearing impaired" was created by hearing professionals which separates "deaf" from "hearing impaired" people. Hearing impaired is generic and includes people with all types of hearing loss. Now, those who identify themselves as "hearing impaired" seem to use the term "deaf" to mean a person who is culturally Deaf, does not speak, cannot hear at all, or is from a deaf school. Hearing professionals who work with deaf people often

impose their hearing values (such as "hearing impaired") on deaf people. They use the term, "hearing impaired" to apply to deaf people who are from mainstreamed schools, can talk, can hear some, or are not culturally deaf...

Social identity is related to both the developing sense of belonging a person feels as part of a group and to being accepted by the group. Robert, a recovering Deaf man, comes from a large Deaf family. While attending AA meetings with other deaf members, he met a recovering deaf woman, Andrea, who is now eight years sober. Andrea became deaf when she was in her early twenties, and is working as a social worker at a deaf organization. She is very involved with the program and became a good support friend for Robert. Robert likes her, but does not feel completely comfortable with her because she is not the same kind of a deaf person as the members of his family. She does not use ASL fluently, and she feels that English is her first language. Although she understands and supports Deaf culture and ASL, Robert feels that she can never be fully accepted in the Deaf world because she has been hearing most of her life. She is different.

A deaf person claims that she is deaf and belongs to a group of Deaf people, but Deaf people reject her for various reasons: attitudes, inappropriate behaviors, or group norms. They may even label her "Hearie" or "Heafie." "Hearie" or "Heafie" labels all types of deaf people who act or think like hearing people. ...More and more young deaf people seem to be marginal, not fitting in to any group of people. If their language identity is ambivalent, and their self-identity is ambiguous, then their social identity is marginal.

(*Conference Proceedings of The Next Step: A National Conference Focusing on Issues Related to Substance Abuse in the Deaf and Hard of Hearing Population, July 5-8, 1992,* Gallaudet University Publication, p. 199-201.)

Cultural Obstacles to Recovery

Deaf people usually look to others in the deaf community for support. However, even in areas where there is a relatively large population of recovering deaf people, there never seems to be enough for a critical mass. There are only a small number of deaf people who are in recovery, and their recovering needs vary greatly. Deaf alcoholics will want to attend AA meetings, Al-Anon members have their own meetings, deaf NA members have other meetings, while African-American deaf AA/NA members want to attend African-American meetings. The impact of cultural differences can take away attention from the real purpose of AA. The real focus is to stay sober, and to try to support others to achieve sobriety through sharing their experiences, strength and hope. Once started on the path to recovery, deaf people may find they have to ignore accepted norms of Deaf culture, such as fluency in ASL or attendance at a residential state schools for the deaf, in order to create a support network.

It is strongly recommended that mixed d/Deaf AA groups establish three general rules:

1) The goal of meetings is to stay sober and help others to achieve sobriety;
2) There will be no judgement nor discussion about Deaf culture or deafness in meetings, and;
3) Confidentiality will be rigorously observed to ensure privacy in the small d/Deaf world.

When a situation requires changes, cultural priorities may have to be set aside. When a Deaf person chooses sobriety, it is not only a matter of making the decision to leave behind old Deaf friends who are still involved with alcohol and drugs. It also means reaching out to new deaf and hearing AA friends. The cultural shock may be significant. For example, Jody, who is in recovery, was trying to develop and improve her self esteem by talking about her accomplishments and other positive things that happened to her. Other people in recovery, understanding this, gave her a lot of support and encouragement.

However, if she shared these stories with her Deaf friends in the community, they might accuse her of being on an ego trip. Humility is highly valued in the Deaf community. It is not considered appropriate to brag about yourself or set yourself above others. For Jody to talk about herself as an individual in AA meetings, instead of as an equal part of a team, may create challenges to her perceptions of self. These cultural conflicts are painful and confusing, and can only be resolved over time.

The Trust-Mistrust Phenomenon

To become independent and self confident can be difficult and slow for many recovering deaf people. They are not only powerless over alcohol and drugs, but also feel powerless over people, places and things. If they are with deaf people, they may be appear competent or even superior. But when they are with hearing people, they may change their behavior and become more dependent with "helpers" and/or "oppressors" who cannot be trusted. They feel ambivalent, and are often reluctant to interact with new people. Another big factor in Deaf culture and the Deaf community, which discourages many people from reaching out for help with their addiction problem, has to do with the trust-mistrust phenomenon.

One of the characteristics of addicts, including deaf people, is that they do not trust anyone. Dr. Barbara Kannapell explored some commonalities among deaf people with this characteristic in her article on the trust-mistrust phenomenon in *Mental Health, Abuse and Deafness,* published by the American Deafness and Rehabilitation Association (ADARA), 1983. She identified several factors why Deaf people seldom come forth and seek help for their alcohol and substance abuse problems:

Deaf people are fearful of "Deaf gossip" and broken confidentiality. If helping professionals are involved in the Deaf community, will they maintain confidentiality? They may not be discreet and inadvertently reveal private matters to other professionals such as a client's teachers or to parents. If the professional is not a member of the Deaf community, Deaf people may feel safer, but then there are questions about the interpreters who facilitate communication in these sessions. Even though interpreters are bound by an interpreter code of ethics, Deaf people sometimes wonder whether or not they are able to refrain from gossiping about what is going on.

If the counselors are not skilled in sign language or knowledgeable about Deaf culture, there may be a serious communication problem that the professional may miss. For example, some deaf persons will have sessions with a hearing counselor without an interpreter. They may insist on speaking for themselves even when their speech is difficult to understand. Deaf clients who are able to lipread may try to get by, catching as catch can and guessing the rest. They even "nod" their heads indicating they understand what the counselor is saying and never admit that they did not understand fully. Other times, client and counselor will communicate by writing notes back and forth with paper and pencil, but for many deaf people, English is a second language. Written English may not convey important connotations and subtle feelings. Incidents such as these may cause confusion for both the counselor and the deaf client, and miscommunication may lead to misunderstanding of the whole process.

Many hearing people in helping professions lack information or sufficient understanding about Deaf culture. Some of them may not know enough to realize that they do not know anything about deaf people. They may try to hide their ignorance by avoiding contact with deaf people outside of the caregiving situation, and try to force their deaf clients to communicate on their terms.

Because of their past experiences, some deaf people have internalized a negative concept of self even before they developed alcohol or drug problems. To them, hearing people are simply better and smarter than deaf people. This attitude may interrupt or slow down the process in counseling sessions between a deaf client and a hearing professional. The process becomes so slow that deaf clients cannot make progress at the same rate as hearing patients and may not be able to accomplish their goals during a brief in-patient stay, such as a 28-day treatment program.

A deaf client may also present different and more positive behavior in front of a hearing counselor, just to impress him/her. The hearing counselor may not be able to detect innuendoes in the client's signing or identify some of the issues important for the recovery process. Furthermore, the deaf client may have poor sign language skills and use incorrect signs just as they may use the wrong English words.

There seems to be what we call a CHAIN-REACTION that occurs in the deaf community. If deaf people know that the services are good, they will FLOCK to them. If services are LOUSY, very few will show up. (Words in all caps are sign language gloss — used to create a specific sign image in the minds of readers who know ASL.)

In other words, if the counselors are deaf or hearing people with fluent ASL and some sensitivity to Deaf culture, deaf people will assume that they also have good counselling skills and spread the word about these services through the deaf grapevine. Deaf people will seek out these providers. However, if one or two deaf clients have bad experiences, they will let their friends know, and then the number of deaf people attending these sessions will decline rapidly.

These and other incidents occur frequently and increase the mistrust between the deaf client and hearing professionals. Memories and stories of bad experiences linger and prevent deaf people from reaching out for needed assistance with alcohol and substance abuse. Although these problems were identified more than fifteen years ago, they remain unsolved today.

Community Reentry

To deaf people who have been in recovery for several years, news that someone has stopped abusing alcohol and/or drugs is terrific. But those in the larger deaf community appear to feel that this is confidential and not to be talked about. Sometimes to the newly sober persons themselves, the news is shameful until they have developed better self-esteem. They do not want others to know that they are having a serious problem with alcohol and drugs. And yet, others in the deaf community have often been aware of the abuser's problem with alcohol or drugs for many years and tolerated it. Ironically, the "shame" of addiction is often attached to those known to be in recovery, rather that to those still abusing. Some deaf people who are in recovery may be skeptical about their own problem and decide that they do not want others to know, so they will perhaps have a drink or two without causing questions among their friends. Some deaf people in recovery refuse to go to all-deaf meetings because they feel that their confidentiality will be violated, and they don't trust the deaf people in the group not to talk about them — especially deaf newcomers. Personal news, both good and bad, about deaf people spreads throughout the Deaf community fairly rapidly. Because of this, deaf people entering recovery often withdraw from the community to avoid shame and embarrassment. They even try to attend hearing AA meetings and bring their own interpreters, paying for their services. They don't want other deaf people to know about their addiction or recovery. For the same reasons, the deaf community often denies alcoholism and drug abuse in its members. The recovering deaf person feels the stigma of alcoholism and addiction in the Deaf community.

   Recovering deaf people are often so ashamed of their past behavior while drinking or using that they will quit the sports teams on which they've been playing or stop going to deaf club events. The Deaf community is so small that "everybody knows" about the problem. Members of the Deaf community tend to cherish past experiences and maintain the past as part of their cultural history. If a recovering deaf person runs into some of her old friends from the past, they may express some doubts that she has changed even though she has been sober for a long time. Members of the Deaf community cannot forget her past or her bad behavior. It seems this obsession with the past, even if it is negative, is part of Deaf culture. If so, it may hinder the recovery of deaf people who may not be given a chance to prove themselves as long as they attend the usual deaf events and activities. It may hamper or even confuse them further about their identity and status as deaf persons.

Minority Deaf People in Recovery

Because the Deaf community is small, there are often recovery groups that involve all kinds of deaf people. Nevertheless, many deaf people tend to turn to others of their race for support. Recovering African-American deaf people usually contact only each other for support. They may sometimes invite deaf people from other races to sports events or picnics, but this interaction, for the most part, is limited to social activities.

Hispanic deaf people with alcohol or drug problems may retreat into their birth families. Closely-knit families will care for their family member and try to watch over them because of their "handicap." Although the intention is to help, this protectiveness prevents deaf persons from turning to other deaf members at AA or NA meetings and taking responsibility for themselves.

An African-American Deaf Person in Recovery

This story is based on an interview with a African-American deaf man who has been sober for seven years.

Out of the many African-American deaf persons who attended an inpatient and outpatient program in a city largely populated by African-American people, Frank was the one who remained sober. Frank grew up in the city and attended a deaf school. He began using marijuana and alcohol heavily in his early teens and continued during his high school days. After graduation, he remained involved heavily with drugs for several years. Eventually he decided to attempt a drug-free life and found the courage to seek help. With a deaf addiction counselor's support, he entered an inpatient program that provided interpreters. When he completed the inpatient program, he participated in a full year of aftercare at the treatment program, which included weekly group meetings. He also had his weekly counseling sessions with the deaf counselor. He received his first year "certificate" for successfully maintaining his sobriety. He continued to attend interpreted meetings and deaf group meetings regularly.

To maintain his new drug-free lifestyle, Frank needed to find new deaf friends who were sober for support and friendship. He learned that all his African-American deaf friends who tried to get sober during his early years of recovery had gone back to drinking, drugging, and dealing. He had several relationships with African-American deaf women, but they did not understand the process of recovery, so the relationships were mostly superficial. His girlfriends were jealous and did not want him to leave them home alone so that he could attend meetings. Nevertheless, he was determined to maintain his sobriety no matter what.

While he was taking care of himself, he was also looking for work. The vocational rehabilitation counselors were very slow in assisting him to obtain a permanent job. Meanwhile, he volunteered to give presentations to groups of high school deaf students at various schools and programs for the deaf. He later made a remarkable presentation at a Substance Abuse Conference that he permitted to be videotaped and used for substance abuse prevention classes.

Frank had a hearing family that stood by him and supported him with love and care. His two sisters were also in recovery and had often been supportive of Frank; however, because they had never learned sign language, the communication Frank had with them was always limited.

Frank's old friends did not have same the strength and determination to maintain their sobriety that he did. They needed more support but were unable to make new friends with the mostly white people who attended AA activities in the local area. Frank tried to attend a church with some of these African-American friends. He did not like the minister, who was white, nor did he feel comfortable with the minister's approach, which Frank thought was oppressive and authoritarian. He refused to tolerate this.

Depending on your point of view, Frank was either doubly handicapped or doubly oppressed by being deaf and African-American. The white deaf community, in general, did not include him or other African-Americans in many activities in an intimate and friendly way unless they were good athletes. At the deaf club, Frank sensed there was a line dividing the deaf white people and himself. He realized that this had been going on for a long time. The white deaf people welcomed him but never made friends with him. Sometimes it seemed okay for him to be there at the club, but inevitably he ran into an invisible glass wall. Frank tried to befriend a new group of African-American deaf people in another area. They did not welcome him immediately. Some of the reasons might be that they had better ASL or English skills and many of them held professional level jobs. Frank was frustrated because he could not address all of these concerns with the deaf people in his community.

What does this story indicate? This is a true story. Even today, there are still very few well integrated deaf clubs and organizations. Much work needs to be done regarding deaf people with diverse racial or ethnic backgrounds. There are questions about whether current history and studies of Deaf culture and American Sign Language include deaf people of color.

Such discrimination was not helpful in supporting Frank in his process of recovery and growth to become a proud deaf citizen in his community.

Gay and Lesbian Deaf People in Recovery

The hearing gay and lesbian community has often shown more support and friendship towards deaf people than the hearing straight community. Perhaps because they have greater understanding about "outsider" status, there seems to be more outreach by hearing gay AA members towards recovering deaf people, either straight or gay. They seem to be more accepting and more willing to attempt to learn some sign language to improve their interactions with deaf people. Deaf gay and lesbian people in AA or NA seem comfortable accepting support from hearing gays and lesbians. Both deaf gay people and straight deaf people appear to trust hearing gays.

In Washington, DC, the Gay/Lesbian AA Clubhouse successfully obtained funding for sign language interpreting at Gay/Lesbian self-help group meetings. Deaf people, both straight and gay, attend these meetings because they are the only interpreted meetings in the city where they do not need to pay for these services. The Clubhouse even offered a room for an all-deaf AA group. The deaf members who attend are both gay and straight.

Deaf Women and Addiction

The National Institute on Drug Abuse (NIDA) has shown that oppressed groups such as women, deaf people, and people of color are at high risk for becoming addicted to alcohol and drugs. Addiction is primarily a physical disease that affects all areas of a person's life. Women are more easily affected than men, because of the way a female body responds to alcohol. More women than men develop severe addiction problems in shorter periods of time if they begin drinking heavily. Many women with alcohol and drug abuse problems experience abusive lives, failed attachments, and a deep sense of despair. For many women, addiction is related to feeling unloved, unwanted, incompetent and to feelings of low self esteem. Alcohol and substance abuse help to alleviate emotional pain related to the oppression that occurs in their lives.

Recent studies also support a genetic and hereditary basis for addiction. For example, women with a family history of alcoholism that includes parents, grandparents, aunts and uncles who have serious alcohol and drug problems are not predestined to develop alcoholism, but do have additional risk. Addiction impacts all areas of life, including personal, professional, social, financial, home, family, and work. It doesn't matter if the abuser is rich or poor, educated or uneducated, young or old, professional or unemployed, deaf or hearing. Furthermore, when women use I.V. drugs, they are at high risk for AIDS. The majority of women with AIDS are drug abusers or the sexual partners of drug abusers.

Deaf women use alcohol and drugs for psycho-social reasons. They drink or use because it helps them feel that they belong, because they are pressured to do so by peers, because they find that drinking or using will ease life's pain, and because they want to alleviate their addictive craving. Appropriate treatment programs are not readily available, especially to deaf women who are involved with illicit drugs and alcohol abuse. Lesbian deaf alcoholics or drug abusers seeking help may encounter additional barriers to treatment. Deaf women who are lesbians may experience fear and prejudice from caregivers in treatment programs or agencies. Because of the deaf community's homophobia, deaf lesbians may keep their problems to themselves and share only with their partners or lesbian friends.

Deaf women with alcohol and drug problems must contend with many additional pressures. For example, in an article in *People Magazine*, (June 20, 1994), where Donna Ryan, a history professor at Gallaudet University, discussed issues of rape, she claimed that the insularity of the Deaf culture has made it hard for Gallaudet women to come forward to tell their stories. "Part of the difficulty for deaf women in dealing with women's issues like rape involves a fear of trashing the Deaf community. In many cases, the women are afraid of being put down by their fellow students for bringing shame upon the university."

"The Deaf community is small and close knit… If you make a fuss at Gallaudet, you've closed a big door," says Denise Snyder, executive director of the DC Rape Crisis Center, in the same article.

Deaf women face the triple stigma of being "deaf, drunk, and women." As women, they are conditioned to have low self-esteem, experience passivity, compromise themselves, and ignore their own personal needs. Loss of support from the Deaf community can intensify feelings of low self-esteem, isolation, and loneliness. Cultural differences, differences in life experiences, communication problems, language differences, and unresolved issues with family members also must be confronted and overcome on the path to sobriety.

Making Transitions in the Process of Early Recovery

In making transitions during the early part of recovery, positive changes are essential. Sometimes treatment programs and self help meetings strongly encourage recovering deaf people to make new friends who are in recovery. Sometimes recovering deaf people do make friends with hearing people who are in treatment programs, but often these relationships are short-lived because of communication problems or misunderstandings that are caused by the differences between Deaf and hearing cultures. Professionals are often not knowledgeable enough to bridge the gap and often may lack knowledge about deafness, deaf people, and Deaf culture.

Jean Modry offered this advice during her presentation, "Cultural Implications of Treating the Hearing Impaired Substance Abuser," at The Deaf Way Conference held at Gallaudet University, July 9-14, 1989:

> ...many professionals who work with the deaf community do not give a second thought about plucking the Deaf from their culture and submerging them into the professionals' culture (hearing) when rendering services. Many professionals insist on speaking English when "communicating" with the linguistically and culturally Deaf. When two cultures do not speak the same language, miscommunications will occur and the level of mistrust increases. The minority culture develops mistrust towards the majority culture. Hearing professionals from the dominant culture have a tendency to measure the world around them by majority (hearing) standards and derive conclusions from them. It is not an uncommon procedure

to impose these standards on the minority Deaf people. In other words, if a certain treatment evoked a certain level of response within the majority culture, the treatment was considered a success. However, when the same level of response was not achieved with the minority culture, the failure was considered to be the result of a deficiency within the minority rather than a deficiency in the treatment itself.

For example, tests were conducted to measure the hearing culture's levels of self-esteem and norms were developed. Then, these same tests were conducted within the Deaf culture. The conclusions were that the deaf in general, exhibited lower self-esteem levels than those of their hearing culture counterparts. What would these professionals find if they focused on measuring the levels of self-esteem only within the Deaf culture? They may find that the lower self-esteem is actually the norm for the Deaf culture. They may find that this is not a deficiency but a human condition based on their culture.

Deaf Role Models

Another obstacle for deaf people is the lack of deaf role models who are in recovery. Sometimes, deaf people from outside the recovery circle provide support and assistance to a recovering deaf addict. This may create a problem if the recovering deaf addict tries to bring the friend as a visitor to regular AA/NA meetings instead of sending the friend to Al-Anon. The other deaf members of this AA group may become upset or uncomfortable. They do not want deaf people outside of recovery to know they are in the program. Even though the friend is there to support the addict throughout the recovery process, this presence creates a problem with confidentiality among the other deaf participants in the meetings.

Some deaf people do meet a few other deaf people who have been in recovery for a long period of time. Unfortunately, some of these deaf "old-timers" are unwilling to provide support to new deaf members. They may be hiding the fact that they are in recovery for various reasons, such as not wanting members of the deaf community to learn about their problem. They may also fear that this knowledge would affect their jobs or relationships with other deaf friends.

Many recovering deaf people who have been sober for a long time no longer attend AA/NA meetings. The few who do attend meetings may not have resolved their co-dependency issues and may offer "help" to other deaf people in order to meet their own needs for self-esteem. Even when a sober deaf role model is available, deaf newcomers are often distrustful and skeptical, and rarely go to them for advice and support.

When deaf AA/NA members no longer attend the meetings, what are some alternative methods that keep these "deaf role models" sober? They usually become more involved with many other activities and advocacy work within the Deaf community. Although they no longer attend AA/NA meetings regularly, they will come to these meetings at least once or twice a year as to share their experiences, strength, and hope.

For example, Loretta is currently 15 years sober. To maintain her sobriety she needs to keep up with the AA program from time to time. However, during the last several years of her sobriety, she has stopped attending regular meetings. She realizes that she has changed her priorities to be more in line with her day to day activities. In other words, she started doing various activities that she was never able to do during her drinking days. She became more involved with community organizations and committees, volunteering to do some tasks.

Nevertheless, she takes some time and makes the effort to continue contact with her deaf AA friends, as well as developing relationships with new friends who are not involved with drinking or using drugs.

Betty G. Miller

Image

Deaf community members are very protective of the image of deaf people. The substance abuse and alcoholism of individual deaf addicts reflects on the entire group and makes the Deaf community "look bad" or humorous. The community response is often to either ignore the serious problem of alcohol and drug abuse that exists, or to avoid deaf people with severe alcohol or drug problems, feeling that they still cannot be trusted, even if they are in recovery.

It is interesting to note that there appears to be more open support in the community for deaf people who test HIV positive or people with full blown AIDS than there is for deaf people who are being treated for alcohol and drug problems. Deaf people who are HIV positive can be more open about their disease than alcoholics.

Alcoholism and drug addiction can result in shame, rejection, and ostracism from the Deaf community. This is true in spite of the wide variety of identities and experiences represented in the deaf community. Deaf family members deny the existence of the problem. Even in deaf clubs or deaf organizations, the topic is not confronted. It is like the proverbial elephant in the living room that no one acknowledges. With this kind of "head in the sand" attitude, how can members of the Deaf community provide support to recovering deaf people, who want to live a drug-free life but still remain in the Deaf world?

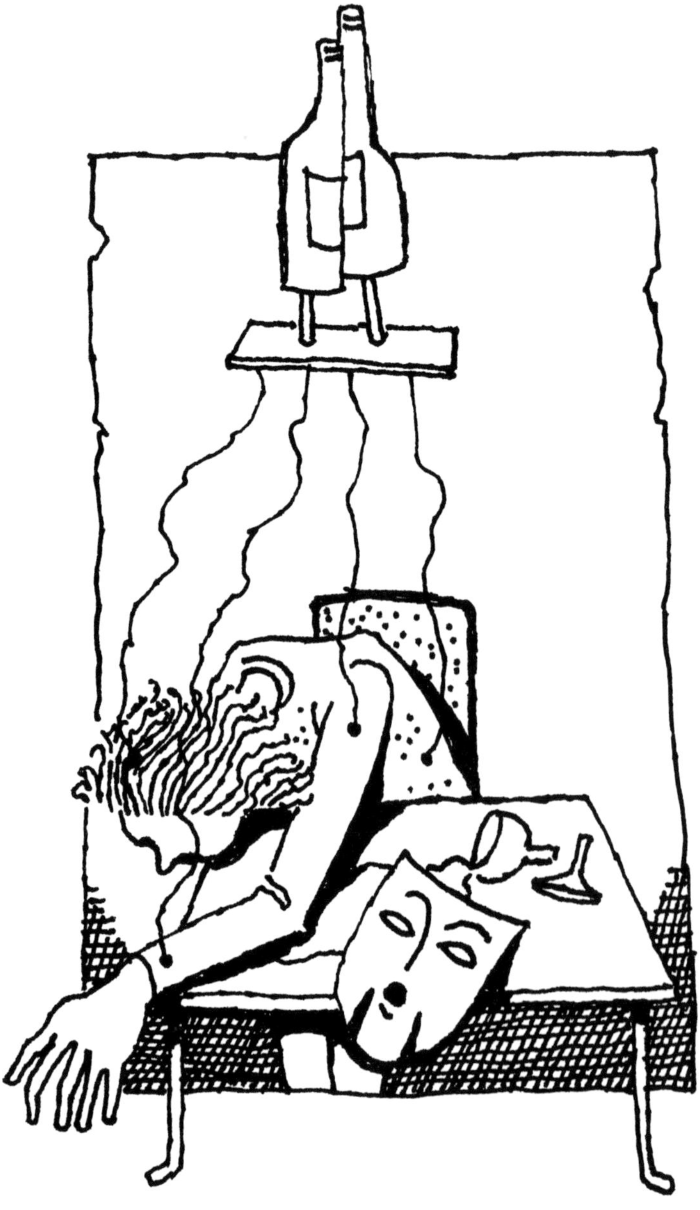

Chapter Three

Treatment Programs: Deaf Units

Jeanne and Ben

Jeanne, who is a deaf professional, was trying to help a deaf co-worker, Ben, who is an alcoholic. Ben was having serious trouble and needed to begin treatment. Jeanne took Ben directly to a detoxification center where the staff referred her to an addiction counselor who is deaf. Jeanne offered to help Ben go through the admissions process, but the staff insisted that the best first step was to contact the addiction counselor, who could then make a professional assessment of Ben and refer him to the most appropriate program.

Jeanne brought Ben to the deaf addiction counselor. The counselor completed an assessment for alcohol and drug use by talking with Ben and using a questionnaire she had adapted for her deaf clients. Ben's answers to many of these questions indicated a serious problem with alcohol, and the counselor recommended that Ben be admitted to the detoxification center. She accompanied him to the detox center, assisted with their assessment, and waited until Ben was finally admitted. She made it clear to the staff at the detox center that Ben will need an interpreter to attend all meetings and counseling sessions during his stay.

The center was unable to obtain an interpreter immediately, and could only find interpreters a few days after Ben's admission to the center. Ben felt quite isolated during his first two or three days while the alcohol was being eliminated from his body, but the doctors and nurses watched over him, helping him with necessary medications. Ben remained at the center for one week, and then he was ready to transfer to a rehabilitation program.

Assessment by Deaf Addiction Counselors

Although some clients seek admission to alcohol and drug treatment programs, most deaf people are referred by a court order, alcohol and drug treatment service centers, deaf service agencies, and other agencies who work with deaf clients. If one is available, these clients are often referred to an addiction counselor who is deaf. During a first session, the client will be asked to complete a questionnaire to help the counselor determine the level of intervention required. Frequently the deaf counselor will adapt certain questions to specifically target deaf issues. The following are some examples:

1) Do you ever wake up in the morning after using alcohol and find that you cannot remember part of the evening, even though after your deaf friends tell you what you did?
2) Do you feel ashamed or worried about what deaf people in the community have heard about your drunken behavior?
3) Do you avoid your deaf or hearing family members or close deaf friends while you are drinking or using?
4) Do you notice that your deaf friends no longer invite you to their parties?
5) Do you feel embarrassed when your deaf friends joke, tease and laugh about your drunk behavior at a party?
6) Are you easily upset when your close deaf friends discuss your drinking or using problems?
7) Do you feel deaf people do not know enough, or do you begin to think hearing people are better than deaf people while you are drinking or using?
8) Do you hide your bottles at home and/or at parties because you think deaf people are MOOCHERS?

If necessary, the questions may be signed and the answers translated from ASL. It is up to the counselor to watch carefully for subtle nuances that indicate deaf issues in the client's responses. Clients may be referred to one of the following types of treatment programs, depending on the severity of symptoms they describe.

Types of Alcohol and Drug Treatment Programs

The alcohol and drug treatment programs to be discussed in this section all have deaf units or are planning to establish deaf units. The author's experience with inpatient treatment programs include seven years in working with a number of programs such as Karrick Hall in Washington, DC. She worked closely with Karrick Hall to develop aftercare plans for deaf patients, and was involved in assisting in the arrangements for aftercare counseling, interpreting, and worked with halfway houses to ensure access and counseling needs of deaf clients were met.

In general, there are three types of treatment options: 1) a detoxification center, 2) a clinical setting, and 3) a social setting.

1) In a detoxification center, the staff includes doctors, nurses, and addiction counselors. The main function of this center is to provide for the physical recovery of alcoholics and drug addicts, sometimes administering medications such as lithium or valium, and helping them to gradually eliminate drugs from their body. The patients are monitored and required to attend group and individual sessions. They are expected to remain at the center for at least five to seven days and are strongly urged to enter a rehabilitation program after leaving. It is not unusual for deaf clients at the end of the detoxification period to leave and not return for rehabilitation services.

Interpreting services are not always provided for these patients. Addiction counselors can negotiate with the Center to make their programs communicatively accessible. If clients are able, the counselor can encourage them to advocate for themselves. One problem that sometimes occurs is that deaf people are not accustomed to seeking professional help from one another. For example, an alcohol or drug-fogged mind may hinder a deaf person's ability to advocate or cause a lack of comfort in working with interpreters who they may know from other deaf community activities.

2) In a clinical alcohol and drug treatment program, the duties of the professional staff and the status of the patient are clear. The clinic staff may include doctors, nurses, psychiatrists and psychologists, addiction counselors, and social workers. The clients are expected to remain in the facility and participate in programs, such as group and individual counseling sessions, for at least 28 days. Each client is assigned to a case manager who has primary responsibility for managing this patient's care.

There are a few inpatient treatment programs in the United States for deaf and hard of hearing patients that are excellent and very sensitive to the needs of deaf patients. They include the Minnesota Chemical Dependency Program for Deaf and Hard of Hearing Individuals, in Minneapolis, Minnesota, and Awakenings in Downey, California. These programs include qualified deaf and hearing staff. Minnesota even includes a program specifically for deaf teenagers.

Inpatient programs, especially those which have deaf units, are usually already knowledgeable about providing sign language interpreters. However, some of them may provide interpreters during limited hours only. For example, interpreting services may be provided during formal treatment sessions and group meetings, but the deaf clients miss out on casual conversations and have no opportunity to interact socially with hearing patients. Much information that hearing clients take for granted is lost, as well as opportunities for bonding and mutual support.

3) In a social treatment model, there is less of a hierarchy. Staff frequently work there to maintain their own sobriety, as well as to assist others. Even the newest resident in a recovery house is expected to make some contribution toward the program's operation. Each resident must take responsibility for the success of the entire group living in the house by developing a relationship with a sponsor and working with other residents and program participants. The addiction counselor, who is not a resident, will be available on a regular basis to provide necessary support.

Programs like these are usually non-profit and funded by clients' insurance, Medicare, or Medicaid. Rarely are there funds to provide sign language interpreters. For this reason, this model may be effective only if the program is for deaf residents. A good example of a social treatment model is a program called Signs of Recovery for the Deaf and Hard of Hearing (SOR) in California.

Intake

Whatever the setting, the admissions procedure can determine whether or not the outcome will be successful. The intake process begins when Jane, a deaf alcoholic and addict, enters a substance abuse treatment program on the first day. The treatment program staff should be prepared for an in-depth, information gathering interview. The questioning and observations should focus on Jane's past and present use of alcohol and drugs, her family history and background, indications and symptoms of substance abuse, and any prior intervention or treatment history.

Jane was referred to a treatment program which is not suitable to her needs. The referral was made by a court order, and Jane's communication preference, learning style, cultural needs, and deafness issues were not considered. Maybe the treatment program is the only one available in the area that can address Jane's drug problem, so the court just assumed that this placement was appropriate. It may be that the staff of the treatment program has very little knowledge about deafness, ASL, and Deaf culture.

An ideal treatment program for deaf people will understand the importance of doing an intake interview specifically designed for screening deaf and hard of hearing individuals. For example, this initial meeting should include an evaluation to confirm Jane's preferred communication choice. This may require qualified American Sign Language interpreting, oral interpreting, or other accommodations to meet her needs. Jane should be gently questioned about life experiences related to deaf issues, such as the types of communication used at home, relationships with hearing or deaf family members, identity issues, and her educational background.

Several considerations must be taken into account when assessing deaf clients like Jane. First, are the staff members conducting the interview knowledgeable about Deaf culture and the life experiences of people who are deaf and hard of hearing? Are they knowledgeable about the various communication styles used within the Deaf community? Second, is the assessor fluent enough to catch the nuances during conversations with Jane? For example, Jane comes from Texas. If the treatment program is in Massachusetts, her signs may differ from local ASL usage. Finally, if the assessor is not fluent in American Sign Language, does she have some in-depth training and experiences in working with interpreters to achieve the best possible results?

These questions are crucial for treatment staff members who wish to obtain as much important information as possible from Jane. The more they are able to understand Jane and recognize critical issues about her deaf identity, ASL and Deaf culture, relating this to her alcohol and drug problems, the more Jane is likely to benefit from this potentially life saving intervention.

In an ideal situation, sections of the intake interview are conducted by a team consisting of the case manager, a counselor, a nurse, a medical physician, a psychiatrist, and a communication specialist. Members of this team may be deaf, hard of hearing, and hearing. Each team member is familiar with deaf issues and has some degree of skill in American Sign Language as well as knowledge about other communication styles used within the deaf community. The average length of time for such an assessment is usually three days, depending on the individual.

During this time Jane has one-to-one interviews reviewing her history for each life area (health, family, legal issues, emotional/behavioral, social, recreational, and spiritual). While assembling this psychosocial history, staff will help Jane identify other possible issues which may need to be assessed further such as depression, signs of abuse, and possible suicidal tendencies. For example, Jane experienced sexual abuse when she was a child, which she has not resolved. Sexual abuse is a common experience among addicted women. The case manager may assign Jane to a personal counselor who will work with her during the rest of the program.

Jane will also be given an explanation of the rules and expectations, and she will be assigned to a buddy or roommate. The results of this detailed information will be shared with the staff, informing the team of Jane's preferred choice of communication and learning style. The main goal of the intake interview is to collect enough data to get to know Jane as well as possible in a short time.

Jane will be given the responsibility of describing her own substance abuse history, which she can complete in writing, on videotape using American Sign Language, or if she wishes, by drawing. Later she will be asked to identify specific feelings in her past and current life. During group sessions, she may be challenged about her honesty by her peers. With the support of her counselor, she will be able to admit to her manipulations and defenses. For example, if she tends to embellish stories in order to make herself look good or to impress others, the group, led by a counselor, may confront her on this character defect, but also assure her that she no longer needs to lie to impress them. In treatment she has the opportunity to practice the honesty which will be crucial to her recovery.

Through working with the staff and her peers, Jane is guided to recognize how her substance abuse has interfered with her family and social relationships, personal growth, and spiritual life. When Jane was drinking and drugging, she went from one extreme to the other. She either became totally passive, keeping to herself, and behaving as if everything was fine; or she became violent and belligerent, attacking her friends, and blaming them for her problems.

If the intake interview succeeds in gathering comprehensive information and identifying her issues, it is possible to determine the best possible treatment process for Jane. With all the data gathered, she may begin treatment and slowly learn to increase her awareness and develop the life skills that she will need so that she can return home. She can begin to recover and maintain her sobriety in the way that is most helpful and appropriate for her.

Whenever an substance abuser enters treatment, it soon becomes clear that many parts of life have been deeply affected by the disease of addiction. Family problems, financial problems, legal problems, social problems, emotional problems, and health problems abound. For deaf persons, there may be additional issues to consider during the process of recovery. Acceptance of deafness, cultural and lifestyle differences between the deaf and hearing communities, unresolved family experiences, and even language and communication access problems within the treatment program all need to be addressed.

With few exceptions, inpatient treatment programs in this country, even with deaf units, are often unsuccessful in working with deaf clients. The most common reason is that funding is usually insufficient to cover everything. The number of deaf patients is too few to justify the costs to public or private funders. Turnover among staff members of the treatment program means that the new staff, especially hearing professionals, will require training about deafness, Deaf culture, and American Sign Language. Such on-going training is time consuming and often not cost effective to the people responsible for the budget. In addition, there are not enough trained, certified interpreters to meet the needs of deaf clients from diverse backgrounds with different ASL and English skills. Even when the facility employs deaf staff, deaf clients rarely see enough deaf role models.

The following factors need to be considered to assist a deaf client new to recovery:

- Where is the alcohol/drug treatment program located? Is it in an area where many deaf persons live and where deaf support services are available? Are there deaf clubs or other deaf organizations that sponsor group activities in the area?
- Will the treatment program have access to resources related to materials and workshops about the Deaf community?
- Will the treatment program arrange for, and obtain, ongoing training and education about deafness, Deaf culture, and American Sign Language? Often there is frequent turnover among staff members, and new staff will always need training.
- Will the program be willing to hire at least one or two deaf counselors to work with them?
- Will the program ask for advice on the issues related to deafness and Deaf culture and hire a deaf consultant to help with the planning?
- Will the program establish an advisory board for the deaf unit and require that 50% or more of the board members be deaf and hard of hearing?
- Will the program include technical devices to accommodate deaf patients in the facility? This includes TTYs, TV captioning and captioned educational films, flashing signals for doors and fire alarms, and sign language interpreters when needed.
- When deaf staff are hired, will there be support provided for them?
- Does the program have access to interpreters who are qualified and trained in alcohol and drug abuse?
- Has the program prepared some activities such as cap-

tioned videotapes and/or other activities in case the scheduled interpreters cannot show up as expected?

• Is the staff prepared to assist clients in dealing with the pitfalls that will confront them in aftercare when they leave the program?

• Is the program familiar with the Americans with Disabilities Act (ADA) and prepared to fulfill the requirements to accommodate deaf clients, as well as to help advocate for other services as part of their aftercare planning?

• Will hearing and deaf family members be included in the treatment plan? What about extended family members such as long-time and close deaf friends?

A Social Model Recovery Program of Deaf and Hard of Hearing People

An example of a social model program that appears to work effectively and successfully is a recovery home for deaf and hard of hearing people. Signs of Recovery (SOR), which was founded in 1986 in Santa Monica, California, grew, by 1995, into a 14-bed treatment facility. They are committed to a recovery home that is free of communication barriers, sensitive to the special needs of deaf and hard of hearing participants, and focused on a 12 Step recovery process. The program provides at least a six month stay in the treatment facility. The home is supported mainly by the deaf residents with their public assistance earnings (such as SSI and SSDI), plus some donations and grants. All direct services are provided by deaf staff. At least five deaf staff people work with the recovering deaf people.

SOR works in cooperation with Community Living for Alcoholics by Rehabilitation and Education (CLARE), which has been providing services to alcoholics and addicts for over 20 years. SOR was originally funded by CLARE through grants. CLARE staff provide guidance and support services such as career opportunities, rehabilitative services, and several other aftercare activities. SOR has a Board of

Directors composed of deaf, hard of hearing, and hearing allies, which acts in an advisory capacity to Signs of Recovery and the CLARE staff to ensure that the needs of deaf people are met.

There is an all-deaf 12 Step meeting on a weekly basis in a location near SOR that is attended by approximately 30 to 40 deaf members. Half of the members attending are from SOR. Others are from other deaf treatment facilities, "alumni" — not only from the Los Angeles area and Orange County, but also from as far away as San Diego and San Francisco. In addition to this meeting, there are many interpreted meetings a week in the L.A. area. Interpreters are funded by the L.A. County Alcoholism Bureau.

Substance abuse programs need to start with what the deaf community has and build on that. The community includes the existing rehabilitation programs working with deaf persons, interpreter referral agencies, deaf organizations, deaf agencies, clubs for the deaf, extended deaf family members, and churches with deaf parishes. All of these need to be looked into when planning how to best meet the needs of deaf people who are ready to confront their substance abuse problems.

There is also the support of volunteers, new friends, and 12 Step sponsors who are deaf and hearing readily available to these newly sober deaf people at meetings.

What is ideal is a circle that includes AA/NA meetings, treatment programs of deaf people, a number of trained addiction interpreters, and recovering deaf persons with long period of sobriety, plus interested deaf friends dedicated to supporting deaf people in recovery.

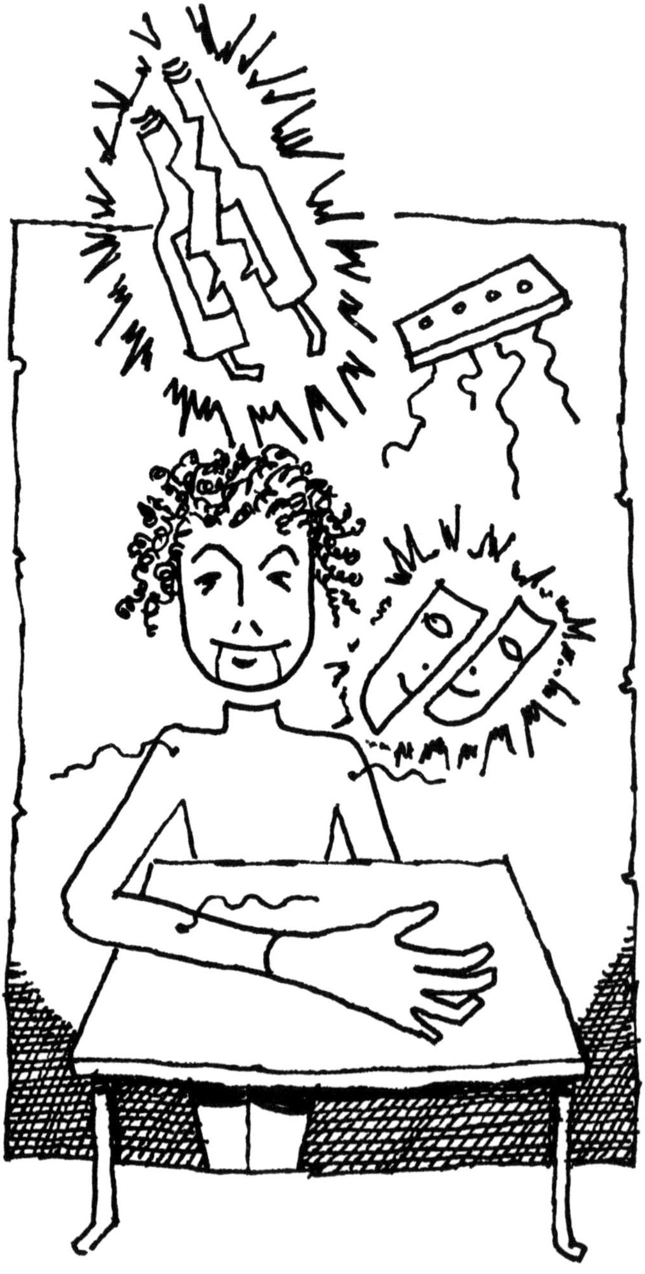

Chapter Four

Aftercare and Beyond

Jon's Story

After Jon completes an alcohol/drug treatment program, he wants to attend as many interpreted AA/NA meetings as he can. He is now back in his home area and has entered the aftercare stage of the recovery process. The treatment program does not provide interpreting services during aftercare, except for a weekly outpatient counseling group. Jon tries to maintain his sobriety to the best of his ability with limited access to aftercare support systems.

Jon is having difficulty obtaining interpreters for his AA/NA meetings, and he feels that this indirectly delays his recovering process. There are not many interpreters available in his area, and some of them are not interested in interpreting AA meetings. Furthermore, some members of the AA/NA groups do not feel comfortable having interpreters (who are usually not AA/NA members) in the meetings.

Jon reads AA/NA books and other literature every night, and tries to find a sponsor to support him through recovery. When he finds a hearing AA member who is willing to make the effort, Jon meets with him face-to-face on a weekly basis to discuss the Steps and learn how to avoid relapses. Sometimes he contacts the sponsor daily through a TTY and relay service. Jon works hard to understand the 12 Steps of Alcoholics Anonymous, but he ignores the 12 Traditions which he feels are not important to his recovery. He is able to work through the first three Steps during his first year of sobriety, although he occasionally attempts the 12th Step by recruiting other deaf people into the program, so that he will have someone to communicate with easily.

Jon is determined to stay sober, and feels good about this. Faced with such limited access to many support systems, he sometimes finds himself wondering if all his efforts are worth it. But he knows he needs to make changes and develop new skills for coping with work, relationships, and every other area of his life. He will have to keep on reaching out for help to maintain his sobriety.

What is Aftercare?

Aftercare is an umbrella term for any ongoing program for substance abusers after discharge from an alcohol/drug treatment program. The goal of aftercare is maintenance. Most recovering alcoholics and addicts must continue to work on their attitude and behaviors and make substantial changes in their lifestyle to prevent relapses and stay sober. The support of a regular program, especially during the first year of sobriety, can be a great help. The program may include daily AA/NA meetings, other workshops related to recovery, and individual and group counseling sessions. Unfortunately, recovering deaf people often encounter language and cultural barriers and limited access to support.

Treatment programs that assign counselors for weekly aftercare sessions during the early months after discharge may not provide sign language interpreters for AA/NA meetings. Sometimes they do not even provide interpreting services for the recovering deaf person in the counseling sessions. Recovering deaf people, using their insurance benefits or paying out of their own pocket, may attempt to find counselors outside the program who are fluent in ASL and knowledgeable about deaf culture. These counselors, however, may not be knowledgeable about substance abuse or the impact of alcoholism and addiction on their clients.

Early Stages of Recovery

Most addicts, like Jon, will pass through distinct stages of recovery. The process requires time and commitment. In order to make changes in his behavior and maintain his sobriety, Jon must begin work on self-concept building skills, with the understanding that he needs to stay sober while practicing these skills. Many addicts have a hard time remaining sober during the first few months of the skill-building process. Some members of AA rely on mottos as reminders, such as "keep it simple," "one day at a time," and "one step at a time." Addicts will need support, especially during the early stages of recovery, to successfully develop these skills, including help from professional services such as individual counseling and vocational rehabilitation.

Self-Concept Building Skills

Substance abuse often arises from a genetic disposition along with a history of neglect, inconsistency, and poor socialization. The self-concept building skills listed below are usually further underdeveloped in recovering addicts because of their alcohol and drug abuse. Addicts use alcohol and drugs to cope with any life situation, good or bad. To learn new coping skills and make positive changes in behavior requires time, effort and practice in the following areas:

- decision making skills
- drug differentiation skills
- stress management skills
- relationship building skills
- help seeking skills
- coping skills
- sexuality and intimacy
- empowerment

There are many good books and articles dealing with these issues. Here, we will look at how deaf experience and deaf culture may affect the development of these skills.

Decision Making Skills

Many deaf people have a history of having decisions about their life choices made for them, long past the age when most hearing children begin deciding things for themselves. These decisions are usually made first by (hearing) doctors, audiologists, and educators who influence and advise hearing parents and family members on what is best for their deaf children.

Very often the doctor or audiologist who makes the diagnosis has been trained in the medical model and holds a pathological view of deaf people. Instead of introducing the family to the deaf community, hearing parents of deaf children are referred to specialists for lessons in lipreading and speech training for their child. They may be warned against using any kind of manual language or even gestures to communicate with their children. Based on this advice, parents make decisions which have long-lasting impact on their children's lives.

Although many deaf children fail to learn speechreading and are unable to speak clearly, some educators and parents persist with the "oral method" (learning through speech and lipreading) and refuse to consent to "manual" classes where sign language is permitted. The children may know that the decisions made for them are wrong, but their protests are usually ignored. This means that the child grows up without a sense of well-being or power over his/her own life and without practice in decision making.

When this "inner child" begins recovery from substance abuse as an adult, decision making skills may be rusty or warped from lack of use. The "inner children" who grow up with no encouragement or support for these skills often do not trust themselves to make choices. They become confused and seem to have an inability to make any decision and follow through on it. They do not know or understand that they have the right to make decisions about how to live, and they fear that any decision they make will turn out to be the wrong one. They have internalized the suggestion that hearing people know more and have the power to make decisions, not deaf people. They have also learned that drinking and drugging help them to deal with these indignities. When they begin recovery, they are confronted with the realization that they need to learn how to make decisions and become more responsible for themselves.

A recovering deaf addict, Anne, ignores the advice of her deaf friend, Irene, because she feels that hearing people know more. She goes to Kathryn, a hearing woman, who offers the same advice using different examples. Anne believes that Kathryn's suggestions are more correct and appropriate, even though Kathryn's recommendations are the same as Irene's. This negative attitude may slow down or confuse Anne's process of learning how to trust herself and make her own decisions. It may also be reinforced by unconscious biases on the part of hearing AA members or professional service providers. Professional providers who work with deaf people often regard their limited ideas about deafness, language, and deaf culture as truths, and then offer advice about what deaf people can or cannot do. Many recovering deaf people follow these recommendations and make decisions based on poor advice. Recovering deaf people in the program are encouraged to make decisions and choices for themselves, and at the same time, are discouraged by the attitudes of the hearing world. This may be a hindrance all through the recovery process.

Drug Differentiation Skills

Some deaf people miss out on public knowledge and may not know the difference between drugs, medication and vitamins. Unfamiliar medical terminology or the incorrect use of ASL vocabulary can be misleading and fail to convey the appropriate concept or information. Like recovering hearing people, deaf people often lack the basic chemical knowledge that addiction counselors take for granted. Furthermore, they may not understand that chemicals can interact with and contradict each other. Counselors must educate their clients about the physical and mental impact of the various categories of "drugs." In doing so, they must make sure they are using correct ASL signs for different drugs.

Betty G. Miller

Anthony goes to a treatment program which has been giving him vitamins to take every day. When he sees a deaf counselor, he tells her he is taking "medication," using the sign MEDICINE. The counselor asks him for the name of this medication, but he does not know. When she calls the hearing counselor at Anthony's treatment program, she finds out that the MEDICINE is actually vitamin pills. The counselor shows Anthony the correct sign for vitamins and explains what they are for and how they differ from medication.

Many signs in ASL that are used for drugs have both positive and negative meanings. For example, a sign for a pill, such as an aspirin, vitamin, or heart medication, is different from the sign for amphetamines and tranquilizers. Some counselors may not know there are different signs in ASL for "good" and "bad" pills. They also may not know all of the new signs, including slang signs, that have been invented for different drugs and alcohol. Some vocabulary depends on where the recovering deaf people are from or who their deaf peers are. These are new signs or modulations of signs that enter the language the same way new words become part of English. We're not talking here of pseudo signs invented in professional settings, but of signs evolved by deaf users to describe various aspects of their real lives.

ASL does not have a sign for the concept of ALCOHOL that extends to indicate alcoholism. The sign usually used for ALCOHOL actually means WHISKEY. This can lead easily to miscommunication. For example, a counselor may be surprised that deaf people do not think that there is much alcohol in beer or wine. On the other hand, Kevin, a recovering deaf person, can't understand why the counselor tells him that there is WHISKEY (in sign language) in beer and wine, when his taste buds tell him differently.

There are different signs for all the various types of alcoholic beverages such as BEER, WINE, WHISKEY, VODKA, and SCOTCH, and for all the different drugs — ACID, POT, COCAINE, CRACK, HEROIN. It's essential for the counselor to know and use appropriate signs for alcohol and for drugs and to be able to convey the whole spectrum of substance abuse, especially those signs that relate to the drug that is being abused.

Counselors who are learning ASL need to become aware of the appropriate signs for this terminology and also continue to keep up with new signs that may develop in various parts of the country. Counselors must be clear about the difference in ASL between VITAMINS, MEDICATIONS and DRUGS because many of these signs are created locally and are often not the same as the signs used nationally. Service providers need to be aware and learn how to sign the concepts in a way that will separate various categories of alcohol and drugs.

Stress Management Skills

One of the first thing to remember about a recovering deaf addict like Joe is that he is already consumed with negative thoughts about himself. He is already stressed from the withdrawal symptoms, such as paranoid thinking, resentments, distrust, making up stories and lying, guilt, fear, confusion, difficulty in making decisions, and cloudiness of thoughts.

Joe bounces between periods of depression with anxiety and crankiness, and positive periods that are like a natural high. He is under heavy stress, experiencing a roller-coaster ride with his feelings going first high, then low. He is also going through grief during his withdrawal. Nevertheless, his counselor, who should be helping him cope with his stress during aftercare, expects him to move on and help out by finding more deaf people for the program. Joe does not feel ready to deal with newcomers who need help with their substance abuse.

At work, Joe, now clean and sober, faces the usual problems in regard to lack of access. There is no TTY in his office, and there are no interpreters provided for staff meetings. He has limited communication with his hearing co-workers because none of his co-workers know sign language. He is increasingly stressed by these frustrations. Prior to his treatment, he had alcohol and drugs to ease his anger and pain, but now, for the first time, he's facing problems at work without the cushion provided by his drinking and drug use.

Joe's emotional state, expectations of others, and problems in his work life are causing tremendous stress. Joe sees a hearing therapist who signs, for help in learning how to deal with his emotions. At work, there is little acknowledgment and support from his co-workers, and he receives little support in the deaf community. At AA meetings, Joe has to deal with sign language interpreters who sometimes show up late or not at all. There may be concern about payment for interpreting services. Other times, interpreters may not have good skills, and they may not be able to adequately interpret Joe's expressive signs into spoken English. His loneliness and frustration are severe. These stresses may cause Joe to relapse during his early recovering process.

Jean's Story

A recovering deaf woman, Jean, is a professional who has been sober less than a year. She just got a job in the mayor's office of a small city, and her position focuses on disability access issues. She is working on developing decision making skills in several areas related to her personal life and work.

Jean's boss is hearing and the mother of a disabled child. She has a mission to make this city the most accessible one in the nation for the physically disabled. She does not understand Jean's thoughts and beliefs regarding the needs of deaf people. She wants all services for the disabled, including deaf people, to be mainstreamed, although Jean has tried to explain that having interpreters in hearing meetings does not always provide full benefit for recovering deaf people. Mainstreaming may work for the physically disabled who are hearing because they share the same language and cultural attitudes as able bodied people, but deaf people have other complicated linguistic and cultural issues. Jean feels frustrated because her boss does not seem to respect her judgement or trust her ability. As the conflict escalates, Jean falters, and loses her self confidence. When she realizes there is nothing she can do to change this stressful situation, she decides to leave her job rather than put her sobriety in jeopardy.

Relationship Building Skills

Deaf children raised in hearing families often miss out on the advantages of early language learning and fail to absorb the dynamics of participation in the process of conversation. Many times neither the parents nor the deaf child know ASL. They may communicate through "home" signs, written notes and speechreading. Even if a deaf child from a hearing family goes to deaf schools or attends mainstreamed classes that allow signing, they are often in a hearing environment where they must guess at what is going on in conversations. This lack of direct and easy communication may hinder development of relationship building skills. Even when some hearing family members do learn enough to become fluent in ASL and to develop friendships with other deaf people, there may be other unresolved issues. Now that Lori is sober, for example, she wants to challenge her family members and their ideas about her. She will need to develop relationship skills before she is able to confront her family about the issues of communication and her deafness.

Communication between the recovering deaf person and hearing family members who do not sign can be facilitated by using interpreters for important family meetings or at large family gatherings. At first, some hearing family members may feel uncomfortable with an interpreter present because they feel that what happens in the family is personal and that the presence of a third party is distancing and artificial.

Alice

Alice, a deaf professional woman, grew up in a family with deaf parents and two older hearing brothers. She and her parents have often joined the hearing family members, her brothers, their wives and children, and sometimes cousins without having a interpreter present. Alice's two brothers, Nick and Alex, sign fluently, but they are not in daily contact with deaf people and do not have interpreting skills. Her brothers also have a poor attitude, considering their sister not quite their equal. The dynamics of this family's communication generally leave Alice, who comes alone to the meeting or gathering, talking only with Nick or Alex. Sometimes she is briefed on what is going on with the other members of the family, sometimes not. Alice often finds herself competing with hearing family members for the attention of her brothers and struggling to keep up with what is going on. This leads to a sense of isolation. She feels that she does not really exist as a member of the family, and that she's not really there. Perhaps it's the absence of an interpreter at the gatherings that makes her feel distant and artificial.

One day, Alice arranged a small memorial service for her deceased deaf parents. She invited her brothers, their wives and their young children, along with several close deaf friends. Nick and Alex's wives and children do not sign at all. Alice hired two interpreters to facilitate all communication, which included not only the formal words of the minister, but also the informal conversation before and after the memorial service.

After the service, most of the hearing women in the family got together to catch up on family matters, while Nick and Alex went into another room. The interpreters kept right on working, interpreting all the conversations. Alice participated in this gathering in a way that she never had before. Alice noticed that her niece looked shocked as she realized that Alice's input into the conversation was right on target. Her niece expected the interpreter to sign only if she talked directly with Alice and did not realize the interpreter would translate all the conversations that could be heard. This niece had assumed that her deaf aunt had no interest in family matters. She had never attempted to have the kind of conversations with Alice that she has with her hearing family members. She had also never experienced the kind of equal participation from her deaf relative that she automatically expects with a hearing family member. It is everyone's loss.

Extended Family Members

There are usually problems in the communication dynamics of families with both hearing and deaf members that prevent normal interactions and impeded feelings of intimacy, trust and reliability. During recovery, deaf people who have experienced resentment and anger about their family relationships may cut off all connections with them for a while. They may need to practice relationship skills with other people and develop a deeper understanding of themselves before they are ready to renew contacts and make some adjustments with their own family members.

Deaf people may have a different concept than hearing people about who their family members are. Not only is their family composed of blood relations, but extended family members may also include close deaf friends and companions. Alice, like many deaf people, has adopted some deaf friends as her extended family. These close friends or extended family members can all communicate in ASL, whereas genetic family members often do not. Sometimes these extended family members are schoolmates or college friends. They may fill in the gaps that are missed in hearing/deaf interactions, such as providing advice and counseling, celebrating holidays, doing favors for each other, and enjoying casual time together at social activities, such as bowling or watching captioned videotapes.

It is common in Deaf culture for people to maintain relationships with friends they have known since early childhood. They grow up cultivating a bond between themselves regardless of their disagreements or faults. They plan and participate in activities such as deaf bowling leagues or deaf picnics. Sometimes they perform close family functions such as advising each other about jobs, helping each other with health matters such as going to doctors' appointments, and sharing information about personal problems and financial difficulties. In the following pages, we refer to these relationships as "deaf family."

Shalini is a deaf woman from India whose genetic family members are all hearing, and all living in India, while she is here in the United States. Her extended family consists of deaf Indians, most of whom came to the United States for college. There is Shivani, who she went to school with in India, and Shivani's husband, Kunal. There are also many others in the community — Ashok and his wife, Rupa; Ajay; Himanshu; Ashish and so on. While most of them are friends, Shalini will often say that Ashok and Ajay are like brothers, and Shivani is like a sister to her. They perform "family" functions for each other. For example, Shivani introduced Shalini to her boss, and thereby helped Shalini get a new job; Ajay and Ashok have often driven Shalini long distances to doctor's appointments; Shalini has listened to Ashok's tales of woe in his marriage and given him advice.

Paul and Jim

Paul, like Shalini, has a strong relationship with his "deaf family." The members of the family include his deaf girlfriend, his deaf brother, and all of his deaf friends. Paul is an addict with a long history of drinking and heavy substance abuse. When Paul enters recovery, he faces several problems. First, most of his extended family members are drinking and using. They are skeptical about Paul's recovery, not only because of their own use of drugs and alcohol, but also because of their denial of the seriousness of Paul's problem. To get the support he needs, Paul starts looking for other deaf people who do not drink or use. He tries to make new friends, but because of the relatively small size of the deaf community, many of these people are also resistant to Paul. He is known by his reputation as an addict. Most of these people are not in recovery and do not understand the needs of a recovering addict. They do not believe in Paul's ability to recover.

Paul joins an all-deaf recovery group, but there are still problems in the relationships among the members. The low-self esteem of these deaf alcoholics and addicts, including Paul, continues to erupt in conflicts throughout the first year of their sobriety. This causes more interpersonal struggles and distrust among these members. Because of this, recovering deaf people during their first few years of sobriety may not develop intimate "family" relationships with each other, and instead attempt relationships with the hearing AA members with whom they may feel safe.

This presents a triple bind to Paul: (1) his "deaf family" are all using, so they cannot give him support; (2) the non-using members of the deaf community will not give him the support nor the kind of family relationships he needs because of their lack of trust, lack of knowledge, and lack of understanding; and (3) his recovery group cannot become "extended family members" without more time for personal growth. The pressures of dealing with these problems may prove to be too much for Paul to handle. Without support, he may be unable to developing the relationship skills he needs, and he may eventually relapse.

Jim, on the other hand, was fortunate. His personal situation was basically the same as Paul's, but his "deaf family" members took the initiative of finding out more about addiction and recovery to provide better support. They attended workshops on recovery and support. They even went to a deaf counselor who explained how they could provide emotional support to Jim and avoid their own tendencies to deny and thus enable his behaviors. They understand that there will be differences in Jim's behavior and attitudes as he becomes sober that may make them uncomfortable. Jim, with help of his addiction counselor, first learns to control his negative behavior, and then, with his new relationship skills, works to improve his relationships with these family members.

Help Seeking Skills

When deaf people enter recovery, they must learn to find help because people rarely manage to maintain their sobriety in isolation. However, it is necessary to know the difference between assistance and dependence. Deaf people need to develop skills in seeking and accepting support while continuing to depend on themselves. At the same time, service providers may need to learn more about how to help recovering deaf people without enabling. Many times service providers, such as doctors, nurses, rehabilitation center counselors, social workers, and alcohol/drug treatment program staff do not know what to do with a recovering deaf person.

Treatment programs that are knowledgeable and provide services for deaf people are few and far between. In rural America, such services are generally non-existent. Treatment programs with deaf units need to assist the deaf community and AA groups to develop resources which can offer support to recovering deaf people. Too many deaf people find communication barriers and limited understanding when they reach out for help during aftercare.

Melvin

Melvin goes to his Health Maintenance Organization (HMO) to ask for help with his alcohol problem, and is given an appointment with a psychiatrist. An interpreter is provided for the appointment, and the psychiatrist concludes that Melvin has a serious alcohol problem. However, he does not know where to send Melvin for help. The psychiatrist contacts a mental health counselor in the same HMO who he thinks may know "some signs." Fortunately, this counselor has experience working with deaf people and has some deaf friends, so he is familiar with some resources for deaf people. He refers the client to a deaf agency. This agency has extensive contacts with alcohol and substance abuse services in the area and not only provides assessment and referral services, but also functions as an advocate, working towards full accessibility for deaf clients. In this case, the HMO counselor just happened to know about this agency through his deaf friends. The HMO never encouraged him to develop those resources for their deaf clients.

The point of this example is to demonstrate that whatever help seeking skills the deaf client already has must be augmented by the service provider's own knowledge of resources within the local community. The deaf person is able to seek assistance at the HMO, but the HMO would not have been able to help if the counselor had not developed his own list of resources in the deaf community.

Membership in the deaf community does not always mean that a deaf person knows where to go for help with every problem. This is compounded by the tendency towards denial which is so typical of addiction. An individual may know about the existence of a social service agency for deaf people but not go there because he is in denial about his addiction or because of his feelings of shame or mistrust of other deaf people. When he first attempts to find help, he may go a hearing psychiatrist or psychologist who is not a part of the deaf community.

Many recovering deaf people have negative attitudes about deaf service providers. They feel that hearing people may be more knowledgeable and better educated than deaf people. They may feel that deaf service providers will know too much about them or know too many of their friends. They may fear that providers at a deaf agency can see through them more easily because of the shared language and culture. Or they may simply not like the deaf service provider who they have met socially. For all these reasons, they will often seek help outside of the deaf community first. The danger in this is that hearing service providers who are not knowledgeable about ASL and deaf culture may not be able to provide appropriate treatment or referrals and can hinder the recovery of deaf people who lack important help seeking skills.

Asking for Help from AA and Other 12 Step Meetings

AA and other 12 Step meetings offer a fellowship of men and women who help each other stay sober. The members are willing to give support to anyone who can admit to their problem and ask for help. They have a special understanding because they all know what addiction feels like. They learn how to recover and maintain their sobriety together through meetings, camaraderie, and support through sponsorship.

In AA, members often practice their help seeking skills with the support of other members. In hearing AA meetings, Elisa, a hearing member, is able to learn new skills and try them out. She feels that she can only do this because she is in a place where she feels very safe. Sometimes she tries out a new skill with a few AA friends, before she attempts it at a meeting. Many of her problems are caused by "survival skills" that she developed when she was young. She is alternately too dependent or too independent. In the supportive atmosphere at the meeting, she is able to release a lot of her anger, people pleasing, and other problem behavior. Over time, she learns more appropriate and healthy ways to seek help.

Good help seeking skills are one of the most essential tools for recovery. Hearing newcomers to AA soon learn to ask for help. In the beginning, if Elisa felt desperate, she could ask any AA friend to help her. She could turn to anyone in any AA group for assistance. She did not need anyone to do her the favor of interpreting. If necessary, she could stay after a meeting as long as she and the other members were willing. She found encouragement in AA groups and the support she needed to learn about asking for help.

Deaf AA members do not have this luxury. A few deaf people may hear or lipread and talk well enough to initiate a conversation and share with some of the hearing members, but most are not ready, or do not feel comfortable approaching hearing members either as a group or one-to-one. If interpreters are available at all, they usually arrive at the appointed time for the meeting and leave at the appointed time, no matter what is going on. Deaf people may always feel like outsiders in a meeting of outsiders.

Few deaf members muster enough courage to seek help from hearing AA members. Often deaf people in hearing groups are ignored. However, there are some hearing AA individuals and groups who do make the extra effort to provide support to deaf members. A few people are willing to learn sign language. Others will at least come up to deaf members, offering encouragement, friendship and support.

Kevin

Kevin does not like to ask hearing people for help since it would be through writing, and he thinks that this would be "unfair" to the hearing person. Sometimes he feels that his English is not good enough to write notes. Perhaps he has been told many times not to "bother" hearing people, not to impose his deafness on the hearing. Like other deaf people, Kevin may attend interpreted meetings, deaf-only meetings, or go to non-interpreted regular meetings just to spend time in the presence of other recovering people without understanding what's being said.

Use of a Telephone Relay Service

A recent option for finding help is through the telephone. Since the passage of the American with Disabilities Act, every state in the USA has installed a state-wide telephone relay service (TRS). With the relay service, the deaf person types a message on the TTY to an operator who reads it aloud to the hearing person without a TTY. This operator then relays the hearing person's response via TTY. By utilizing the relay system, recovering deaf people and hearing AA members are able to communicate. All conversations handled by the relay services are confidential, and the text is destroyed after the call.

Increasingly, deaf people who have access to computer technology are also setting up computer conferences instead of, or in addition to, meetings. Many recovering deaf people may feel more comfortable reaching out for help through this new technology.

Providing Support

Recovering deaf people also need to learn how to provide support as part of the process of seeking help. As they continue developing better coping skills, they can learn how to give, as well as accept, support and encouragement. The concept of offering support to other members, especially hearing members, is often difficult for recovering deaf people to grasp. They are more familiar with family-centered giving like helping a friend to move, fix up a new home, repair a car, or lending this friend their car. The concept of providing emotional support to hearing or deaf strangers may be difficult for them. However, in an environment such as AA meetings, they can volunteer for various jobs and offer assistance to other members.

Another kind of service may be for a deaf group to volunteer to go to a treatment center that has a newly sober deaf patient and hold a meeting there. This way they are available to deaf newcomers who need their help.

Jack

Jack, a recovering deaf addict, may view a newly sober person as someone who is immature and who never grew up. The idea of providing emotional support to a person who is acting out, and recognizing that the behavior is a phase of the addiction and recovery process, may be very new to Jack. Making positive comments and providing support in that kind of situation is opposite to Jack's experience in his deaf culture where rules for behavior are strict.

Coping Skills

Veronica

When Veronica, a deaf woman, entered recovery, she learned that she must develop entirely different coping mechanisms to deal with everyday life from what she had utilized during her drinking and using days. While she was still drinking and using, she managed her negative feelings by getting high and tuning out. Now that Veronica is sober, she suddenly finds that she feels emotions with greater intensity, and she no longer can use her old methods of coping. She used to deny any responsibility for her actions or misbehavior. Now that she is sober, she finds that she must face the consequences of her actions without the cushion of intoxication.

Growing up in her hearing family, Veronica seldom experienced the consequences of her actions. Because she was deaf, her hearing family and her hearing friends let her have her way rather than make the effort to communicate with her and try to teach her responsibility for her actions. Now she is sober and finds that not only is she feeling with more intensity, but she is also expected to be accountable for her actions. Like many recovering addicts, she does not know how to do this, nor how to cope while she is sober.

Veronica grew up without really understanding appropriate rules of social behavior. No one in her family signs, so she was allowed to indulge in a lot of bad behavior while growing up. At the time, it seemed easier to give in to her than to try to learn to communicate and teach her to follow the household rules. When she went to a school for the deaf, she had already internalized the attitude that she did not need to suffer the consequence of her actions. At the school, she managed to get away with breaking a lot of rules, although she was occasionally caught at some misdeed and punished. She knew how to win sympathy, so this behavior was never taken seriously. She began drinking more and more often before or after school. Later she used marijuana, and then near the end of her senior year, she became addicted to cocaine.

After graduation from high school, Veronica found a job and began to work, still trapped in her old behavior patterns. She discovered that her boss would not tolerate such behavior. He confronted her regarding her drug abuse problems and told her to either get help or be fired. Veronica was forced to go into a treatment program because she did not want to lose her job.

Veronica's Experience in Learning to Cope at Work

Now that she's sober and has finished her 30 day treatment program, Veronica discovers that she still has her old behavior problems. For example, her boss does not accept her coming in late for work, missing days, or fighting with co-workers. With help of her deaf addiction counselor and her housemates who are also in recovery, Veronica begins to develop the skills she needs to cope with her problems. She lives in a recovering women's half way house. She accepts responsibility for household chores and rules. She gets support from her recovering housemates and shares problems and experiences with them. Within two years, with treatment and support, she finally learns how to behave at work and to accept the consequences of her misbehavior and rule breaking.

Training in coping skills focuses on topics such as the purpose of rules and the consequences of behavior. For example, early in her recovery, Veronica asked her supervisor for an emergency leave for the rest of the afternoon. Her supervisor asked her a lot of questions about the nature of her emergency, and eventually turned down her request because the emergency was simply that Veronica was upset about something personal, unrelated to work. Veronica became angry not only because her request was denied, but also because the supervisor asked her so many questions about the reason for her request. When Veronica talked with her addiction counselor, she realized that the supervisor had a right to ask questions and that there is a work policy she must follow. The counselor and Veronica discussed the reasons for rules and policies at her workplace. She is learning that behavior has consequences and that she is responsible for her own actions, both negative and positive.

Recreational Activities as a Coping Skill

Recreational activities with other deaf people in recovery are an effective strategy for learning to cope. For example, a group of recovering deaf people formed a bowling team and joined a deaf league in their local area. They learned how to improve their bowling skills and cope with the excitement of winning and losing. The same benefits can be found on baseball teams and other sports. Groups of recovering deaf people can gather for an informal get-together in each other's homes, such as a video and popcorn night. Each member can take responsibility for a specific task as the group makes arrangements to help each other have a successful activity. Responsibilities are delegated to each of the members, and the members learn how to deal with mistakes that occur in making simple arrangements. If there are problems caused by some of the members, the group can discuss things and learn from each other.

Learning Coping Skills at 12 Step Meetings

Deaf AA members recognize that they will need to learn many new ways of dealing with their alcoholism and drug addiction during their sobriety. This level of acceptance is necessary at the beginning of recovery. They understand that they need to attend as many AA meetings as possible in the early stages, while they are still coping with withdrawal from drinking and using. Another important resource is frequent contact with an AA sponsor who can offer experience and advice on many issue.

Supportive AA sponsors and friends, who are making efforts to improve their own behavior and cope with their own feelings, often try to assist other members who are struggling with their emotional situations by simply talking with them, sharing their own experiences, trying to be present for them, and accepting them as they are. Many addicts are arrogant, especially while using and drinking, and may have never grown up enough to cope with their emotions. In this respect, recovering deaf addicts are no different from hearing addicts, but they may be subjected to more criticism from other deaf members who do not fully understand that coping is a new skill to be developed.

Developing the coping skills to live without alcohol or drugs takes newly recovering people a long time. It can only be achieved through practice, by doing things such as learning to confront and deal with anger, working on the Steps, and accepting the consequences of bad behavior and arrogance. Developing coping skills also increases self-esteem, with validation coming from counselors and AA friends who understand the whole process.

Sexuality and Intimacy

Young people entering their teen years are challenged by issues of sexual identity, sexual behavior and intimacy. They learn from friends, through trial and error, and hopefully receive some education from their families, counselors, and teachers. But young people who become addicted during their teen years have often stunted their personal, as well as their physical growth. They become dependent on alcohol and drugs to be able to perform sexually. Intimacy is suppressed. What should be a pleasure becomes another aspect of the problem.

It is important for recovering deaf persons to share information and resources about the impact of substance abuse and the recovery process in the areas of sexuality and intimacy. As people recover from chemical dependency, they may need to re-examine their gender roles, their courtship rituals, sexual practices, and related intimacy issues.

Recovering deaf people need to examine techniques for dealing with intimacy in a way that is based on their reality. For example, deaf people often repress the anger they feel toward their hearing parents. They may unknowingly direct their anger inwards or act out their disruptive behavior on their significant other. To make changes in their behavior, they may need to work through these feelings and try, if possible, to resolve some of the barriers between themselves and their parents before they can improve their adult relationship with a partner.

On the other hand, during the early stages of sobriety, a recovering person may behave like a teenager who is experiencing sexuality and intimacy for the first time. He or she may even experience having crushes and infatuations while on a roller coaster of emotions. While it is normal for a teenager to experience these feelings, it is awkward and strange for a 35 year old man or woman to revisit this same period.

Sexual Identity and Sexual Behavior

Recovering persons may experience confusion between relationship problems and sexual identity. In the beginning they may experience little or no sexual desire at all or they may find that their desire for sexual activities increases as a substitute for their substance abuse addiction. They may experience confusion about their sexual identity and wonder if they have suddenly changed orientation. Sexual identity changes or confusion should be discussed and resolved through appropriate counseling.

Susan

Susan, a newly recovering deaf woman, is confused about her sexual identity even after she becomes sober. She has been bisexual for some time, but feels that she is more physically attracted to women. She realizes that she needs to abstain from having sex for at least the first six months of her sobriety. She needs help through counseling to discuss issues and experiences in her past sexual relationships.

George

George, a newly recovering deaf man, is having sex with a girlfriend for the first time since entering recovery. He chooses a hearing woman who is not involved in the deaf community. George is having some difficulty in making love without the props of alcohol or drugs. His girlfriend, who is also an AA member, is supportive and understanding. George deliberately chose a hearing woman because he was afraid that if his partner was deaf, the deaf community might find out about his inadequate and awkward sexual performance. It will take several years of sobriety before he feels confident and able to have a significant and honest relationship with any woman, hearing or deaf. George needs to be careful not to become obsessed with sexual activities, as there may be a tendency for him to use sex to replace his other addictions. If this becomes a problem for him, he is encouraged to attend Sex Anonymous (SA) meetings.

Denise

Denise finds that her deaf male friends are interested in her only for sex. Unfortunately, once a person has a certain reputation in the deaf community, it is hard to leave it behind. The community is skeptical even though Denise has entered recovery. She becomes confused, hurt, frustrated, and angry. Denise learns that not only is she known for her promiscuous behavior, but also for many troubling incidents that occurred in the deaf club due to her drinking and using.

   Her deaf friends and acquaintances are unable to change themselves to deal with Denise as a sober person. Some of her dates no longer want to go out with her. They say she is no longer a lot of fun to be with. They may even feel awkward with her new sobriety. In the past, Denise's friends mistook her actions as promiscuity, when actually she was desperately searching for affection and attention. Maybe she thought sexual favors were necessary to be accepted in a relationship. Whatever the reason, most members of the deaf community lack understanding about the changes she is going through during her recovery and may not be very supportive. Denise may need to make new friends in the hearing AA community and focus on her recovery for the time being.

Intimacy

Recovering deaf people also need to be aware that their past behaviors may alter their present relationship with a longtime partner. The unhappiness of the past may affect the sexual part of the relationship even if the partner is supportive or also in recovery. Painful memories of verbal or physical abuse and resentment over embarrassing incidents in public during the old drinking and using days may surface and need to be addressed. Lack of trust and fear of sexually transmitted disease and AIDS because of past affairs outside the relationship may be very hard to overcome. The changes in behavior and personality that sometimes occur in the early stages of recovery also put a strain on relationships.

For example, Mary finds that her significant other, Bob, is distant from her and unwilling or unable to have sex because he has bad memories of her flirtatious, promiscuous, and sometimes violent behavior with other men at the deaf club while she was drinking and using. Furthermore, there is still bad gossip about her circulating in the deaf community, and he feels very embarrassed and ashamed.

On the other hand, Mary thinks that having sex with Bob will please both of them, but she is not comfortable with intimacy. She feels that if she shares too much about herself and gets too close to Bob, he will reject her in the end. It is much easier to offer sex than to share her inner thoughts and feelings. She thinks this will keep Bob happy.

Developing an intimate relationship makes many recovering people feel vulnerable and requires courage for both partners. Though it is risky, with patience and understanding, intimacy can be achieved. In building their relationship, Mary and Bob learn that they can be close without sex. With patience and love, Bob consistently offers support and understanding. He gives Mary the freedom to be vulnerable and become more of herself, and slowly an intimate relationship develops between them. New, positive experiences enable Mary and Bob to learn and understand more about their life choices and face the difficult changes and decisions required in serious relationships.

Empowerment as Part of the Recovery Process

Personal empowerment is a challenge for many recovering deaf people. First they need to become self sufficient and self confident through education and training about Deaf culture and American Sign Language. This education and training should be provided by deaf leaders and deaf educators. Recovering deaf people need to learn to appreciate themselves and their abilities. During their early sobriety, they can begin to take responsibility by doing simple things such as setting up the AA meetings of their home groups, planning programs for the meetings, and attending business meetings as needed.

They can later move on to somewhat more complicated activities such as planning for a fund-raising event. A car wash on a monthly basis can help with expenses such as interpreting services for other AA meetings. One recovering African-American deaf man, after six years of sobriety, volunteered to share his experiences of alcoholism, drug addiction, and sobriety at substance abuse prevention programs for deaf students. With the help of his counselor and support friends, he sent out letters to several educational programs offering his services as a recovering deaf role model. Eventually, he was asked to come to some of these schools, and made several successful presentations. His self confidence blossomed, and he was able to move on to new responsibilities. For recovering deaf persons like Steve, Bob, Mary, Denise, George, Susan, and others, time, patience, and a lot of personal work is required before they can deal with daily life without endangering their sobriety and confidence.

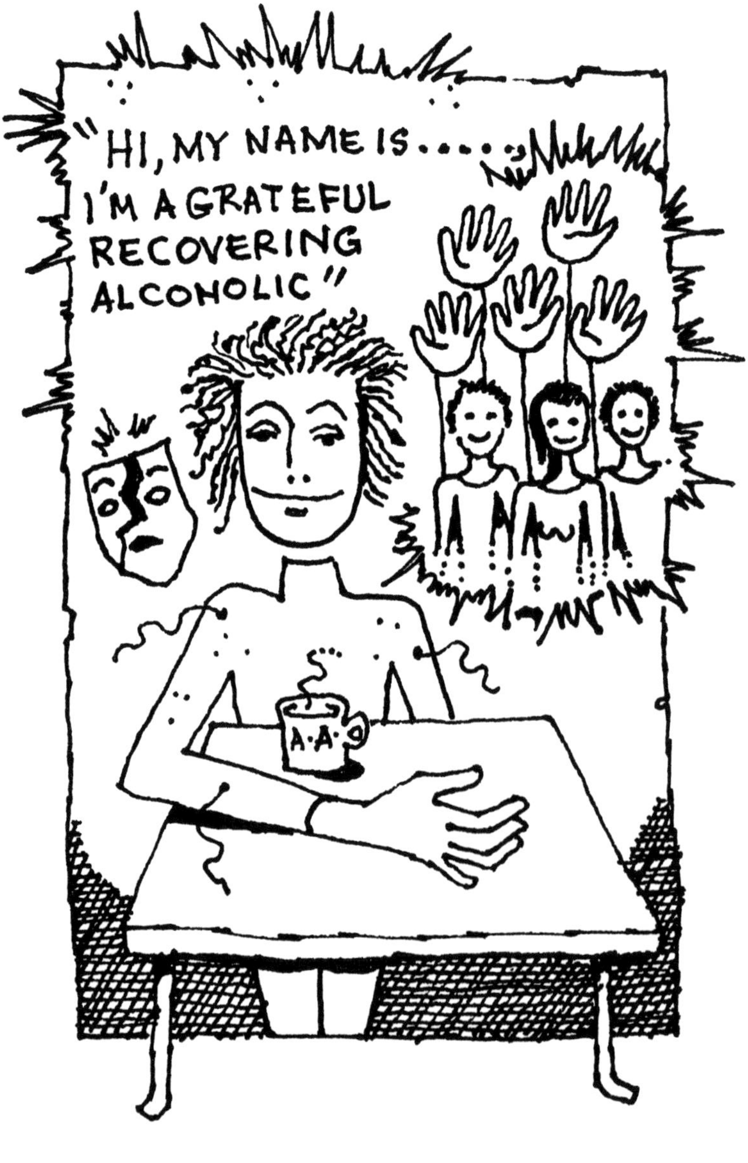
"HI, MY NAME IS.....,
I'M A GRATEFUL
RECOVERING
ALCOHOLIC"
A·A

Chapter Five

Alcoholics Anonymous, Its Twelve Steps and Twelve Traditions

Helen's Story

"Hi, my name is Helen, I am a recovering drug addict." This is the usual introduction that Helen uses when she speaks to share her experience, strength, and hope with other members of Alcoholics Anonymous (AA) during a meeting. She may talk about what her life was like when she was using and drinking or what it is like now that she is sober. Helen tells her story in American Sign Language (ASL). Melissa, a certified sign language interpreter, translates Helen's ASL into spoken English and the words of the hearing members into ASL. It is difficult work, and the members have had to learn to make adjustments for the occasional miscommunication. Communication is easier at the all deaf AA group, but it meets only once a week. Helen attends four to five AA meetings a week, so she can get the support and encouragement she needs to maintain her sobriety. She has found a sponsor in one of her AA groups and tries to do her 12 Step work, so she can make changes in her behavior and maintain her new drug-free lifestyle.

Most of the time she feels comfortable with members of AA, both deaf and hearing. They all share an understanding and common goal, which is to achieve and maintain sobriety. They all understand that they cannot successfully stay sober by themselves. AA friends provide the support Helen needs to keep working on the 12 Steps. She knows that there is no time limit to do all the Steps. She understands that she can probably only focus on the first three Steps during the early phase of recovery. But she also understands that she probably will not be able to maintain her sobriety unless she continues to work her 12 Step program one day at a time. For Helen, recovery will be a lifetime process.

Alcoholics Anonymous

Alcoholics Anonymous (AA) is a world-wide fellowship of alcoholic and addictive men and women who come together to solve their common problems and to help fellow sufferers recover from alcoholism and addiction. AA began in 1935 in Akron, Ohio after a meeting between a surgeon and a stock broker, both severely affected by alcoholism.

Over the next few years, three successful groups emerged — the first at Akron, the second in New York, and the third in Cleveland.

AA's 12 Steps are a group of principles, spiritual in nature, which can be practiced as a way of life. Over time, consistent practice can control the obsession to drink and enable the sufferer to become happily and usefully whole. The basic principles of AA were borrowed mainly from the fields of religion and medicine and modified through years of experience and careful attention to the behavior and needs of members. In 1939, the new organization set down its experience in writing. The book, *Alcoholics Anonymous,* known as "the Big Book," gave the groups a name and became the basic text of the fellowship.

Publication of the book set in motion a period of brisk expansion as recovering alcoholics carried their message of hope to others. Questions of membership, money, personal relations, public relations, management, and the like threatened the stability of the young movement. It was out of this confusion that AA's 12 Traditions took form. They were first published in 1946 and later confirmed at AA's first International Conference held in Cleveland in 1950.

AA's 12 Traditions apply to the life of the fellowship itself. As the organization and its influence continue to grow, the Traditions maintain their current form, substance and unity. They outline the means by which AA relates to the world, the way it lives and grows.

Meetings are the main activity of AA. Meetings may be open, that is, open to all who wish to attend, including family and friends of AA members as well as other outsiders and the curious. Meeting locations, days, and times can be found by contacting AA volunteers at the AA central office in almost any town or city throughout the country. Generally, during open meetings, one or two speakers will share their experience, strength, and hope and try to inspire the same in others. Closed meetings, which are limited to AA members only, may have several different formats. There may be a speaker, a Step group which studies each of the 12 Steps in repeated cycles, study groups focused on various aspects of the Big Book, discussion groups, and other formats.

All kinds of people can be alcoholics or addicts. Likewise, AA men and women may be of any race or nationality, any religion or ethnicity, and almost any age. They may be rich or poor, brilliant or boorish. They may be doctors, lawyers, other professionals, housewives, teachers, janitors, truck drivers, airline pilots, members of the clergy, students, post office employees, homeless, hearing, or deaf.

Deaf people usually find out about AA through friends, TV shows, local newspapers, counselors, local AA offices, and deaf agencies. Sometimes they will contact interpreting services to find interpreters to accompany them to hearing AA meetings. At first, deaf people may not feel comfortable around so many hearing strangers. They may prefer to go to speakers meetings and avoid interacting with hearing AA members. Even when there is an interpreter to provide accessible communication, the whole process of AA meetings can be unfamiliar and awkward for newcomers.

It is not easy to build a bridge between the deaf and hearing worlds, even for fellow sufferers. Some hearing people may learn a few signs, but very few hearing people will become fluent in ASL. Without skill in the language, the lifestyle and experiences of deaf people are difficult for hearing people to understand. Sometimes, however, deaf newcomers take advantage of the language difference. Hearing AA members and professional helpers may feel pity and think the deaf members do not understand AA's principles and purposes or the 12 Step program. They may think it is because of problems with English, when the truth is that the deaf person is unwilling to work them through. Actually, fully understanding the concept and work of the 12 Steps, no matter what language is used, will take several years of sobriety.

Deaf members usually attend meetings at least once a week, depending on the availability of interpreting services. Hearing members will occasionally bring along a friend or family member to a meeting. Deaf members, however, are not encouraged to invite their deaf family or friends. The deaf community is so small that it is difficult to maintain confidentiality. The presence of deaf non-members may cause the regular deaf members to feel uncomfortable and inhibited unless they have had ample warning and the opportunity to give or withhold consent.

AA Sponsors

To be a sponsor, an AA member should be at least five years sober as well as ready and willing to give support to a newcomer. The primary purpose of the sponsor is to help a newcomer stay sober by providing support on a regular basis. A sponsor is not a counselor, but offers support based on his or her experience with sobriety and the AA program. Deaf people can request a hearing or deaf AA sponsor for support. A deaf sponsor is usually the first choice, but this may not be possible because the recovering deaf community is so small. Deaf people who are really serious about their sobriety are willing to work with hearing sponsors and to find ways to communicate and share their experiences. They feel that the issue for them is not deafness but sobriety, and this must be their only focus, especially in the early stages of recovery.

Nevertheless, communication adjustments have to be made in the process of building a relationship with a hearing sponsor. Relay services which permit a TTY user and a voice telephone user to communicate through an operator are now available in all states, but it may take some getting used to for both people, especially when the communication is sensitive. Eventually the hearing sponsor may get a TTY device or the deaf AA member may be able to loan or provide one.

For person-to-person communication, they may use a pencil and pad to write back and forth. The deaf member may teach the sponsor some sign language, or the sponsor may take some classes; however, it takes several years for a new signer to become fluent. For example, the sign for ALCOHOLIC is an "A" handshape which has a quick lateral moment located at waist level near the right side of the person's body. Signing ALCOHOLICS ANONYMOUS is almost the same except that the location of the moment is at shoulder level. Subtleties like this easily confuse new sign language learners and cause translation problems or misunderstandings of whole dialogues. Sometimes an interpreter can be found who is willing to interpret between them for an hour or two. It will require willingness and determination from both the AA sponsor and the deaf AA member to work out their communication, one day at a time.

Deaf 12 Step Meetings

Some all-deaf 12 Step meetings do not follow the normal pattern of hearing meetings. This can be upsetting to hearing people and to deaf people who have not grown up in or been acculturated into the deaf community. For example, most hearing AA meetings begin with a reading, often from Chapter Five of the Big Book of *Alcoholics Anonymous*. Deaf meetings may start out with readings for awhile, but eventually they are dropped by group consensus. This is because when deaf people sign the readings, they are translating them from English to ASL, which becomes time consuming and even confusing. At a hearing meeting, people are often coming in and settling into their seats during the readings. As the language is frozen and unchanging, people can listen with "half an ear." In a deaf meeting, however, all deaf members must be settled in and ready to pay visual attention. With the effort to translate, what takes five minutes in a hearing meeting consumes 15 minutes in a deaf meeting. It's also confusing because each person will translate the English differently — changing the meaning slightly each time.

Sometimes, a videotaped ASL translation of Chapter Five of the Big Book entitled "How It Works," will be shown prior to the beginning of the meeting. This may save time, allowing more time for individual or group sharing in the meetings.

Questions have been raised about whether or not the AA program has been successful for most deaf clients. Some professionals who work with recovering deaf people have even tried to rewrite the 12 Steps into what they consider more basic English. This type of adaptation has not been effective because rewriting can actually change the meaning of the Steps.

Deaf AA members may experience problems in the predominately hearing world of AA and some adaptations may be necessary to accommodate deaf language and culture. Nevertheless, most deaf people who are serious about recovery are willing to work through the 12 Steps.

Fortunately, there are now a few ASL translations of the 12 Steps on videotape. The translations are not exact; however, most of them are adequate and signed by fluent ASL signers. Appropriate translations from one language to another depend on familiarity with the culture of the target language users and full understanding of the meaning of the material. This work is very difficult, but worthwhile in many ways.

Working the 12 Steps

In the following section, the 12 Steps are described through the experience of a hypothetical deaf woman, Gayle, who is newly sober. Gayle is trying to understand the philosophy of AA and to use the Steps to guide her recovery.

Step 1: "We admitted we were powerless over alcohol — that our lives had become unmanageable." What does this mean to Gayle? Take the word "powerless." It is true that recovering alcoholics have no power over alcohol, but Gayle has felt powerless all her life. Since she "failed" her hearing test and was "diagnosed," her parents, the doctor, audiologist, and (mostly hearing) educators have made the important decisions affecting her education and lifestyle. Power, therefore, may have a different meaning to a deaf person than to a hearing person. The paradox is that, in the context of AA, this word "powerless" becomes a positive force enabling recovering alcoholics to let go of alcohol and drugs and learn to live a clean and sober life. When Gayle eventually understands and learns to distinguish between positive and negative power, she accepts that she has no power over her use of alcohol and drugs. The first Step teaches that she needs to let go completely in order to find the strength to go on with life without alcohol or drugs.

What does it mean that "…our lives had become unmanageable"? Gayle understands that she becomes unmanageable when she drinks or uses drugs. But what does this really mean? Her deaf life has often appeared unmanageable to hearing people. For example, Gayle is sometimes noisy in the kitchen. The sound of rattling pots and pans or slamming drawers and cabinets represent unmanageable behavior to hearing people. They may think that Gayle is angry. Many deaf people are taught to try to be quiet in their movements. John, her friend, once shared that for many years he thought that if he aimed at the right spot in the toilet bowl while urinating, he would not be making too much noise. He aimed at the bowl area just above the water level. He later learned that for hearing people, such noises are inevitable, and they do not even think about it. Gayle eventually learns the real meaning of "unmanageable" in the context of deaf culture norms and lifestyle. She has been insensitive to others, self-centered, as well as physically and verbally violent. She has been unable to control her emotions while drinking and using, which includes behaving inappropriately.

Step 2: "Came to believe that a Power greater than ourselves could restore us to sanity." There has been very limited participation in churches "of the deaf" because many deaf people feel that certain church leaders (both hearing and deaf) are too authoritarian and condescending towards the deaf people in their congregations. To Gayle, the word "power" appears authoritarian, and she may feel resistant to the concept of God (especially when someone uses the sign "God") for the "Power greater than ourselves." Gayle confuses spiritual reality, which is an essential part of the 12 Step program, with authority.

"…restore us to sanity." Gayle thinks that the opposite of the English word sanity must be "insanity." Step 2 may mean that she will need to go to a mental health program. In some sign language conversations or even translations of Step 2, the sign for INSANE may incorrectly appear. However, in Step 2, the English word, "sanity" really means maintaining life in a calm and simple way, learning appropriate behavior, and seeking guidance for help to make changes. When Gayle understands this concept, she uses another sign, such as PEACEFUL, to indicate the true meaning of "sanity." From this, she begins to develop trust that AA meetings and other AA members will help her maintain her sobriety and sanity.

Step 3: "Made a decision to turn our will and lives over to the care of God as we understood him." After understanding Step 2, Gayle may be ready to open her mind to make a difficult decision. The challenge is to "let go" and let the "spirit" or "higher power" take over. Again, the issue of power comes up and the implication is that Gayle needs spiritual "help." She learns that "turning it over" is not about authority, which she has struggled with in the past, but about a spiritual faith and hope. She now realizes that she cannot always depend on people, places, or things for support. She tries prayer and meditation to guide her through.

Step 4: "Made a searching and fearless moral inventory of ourselves." Translated directly into sign language, INVENTORY refers to making a list of things in storage or things that are priced for sale. To convey the concept of Step 4, Gayle signs the phrase "LOOKING-INWARD-AT-OURSELVES." With this understanding, Gayle starts to look back on her past behaviors and admit how she hurt other people. For example, does she use being deaf to manipulate other people and get things she wants? Is she jealous or envious of other deaf people who succeed at their jobs or lives? Does she look down on or insult deaf friends who are less educated or less well off? Does she avoid taking responsibility for her life? With all these questions to ponder, she makes a list of her character flaws, using a videocamera, and then prepares for Step 5.

Step 5: "Admitted to God, to ourselves, and to another human being the exact nature of our wrongs." The purpose of Step 5 is to help recovering people rid themselves of their dark secrets and their sense of isolation. Gayle needs to share her 4th Step inventory with someone she can trust. Gayle has been getting to know some deaf and hearing AA friends. Sometimes Gayle does not like to share with other deaf people because of her fear that "gossip" that might spread about her. She may feel "safer" sharing her secrets with hearing people who have no connection with deaf people or the small deaf community. On the other hand, she may choose to share her character defects with one or two trusted deaf friends or a deaf counselor rather than with hearing people. She may be afraid of being judged or patronized by these hearing people.

Step 6: "Were entirely ready to have God remove all these defects of character." Gayle is now ready and willing to make the changes in her behavior that interfere with her personal and professional development and with her relationships. Defects of character have resulted in behaviors which are not acceptable in either the deaf or hearing community. For example, at the workplace, one of the requirements is to be at work on time. Gayle is taking more responsibility for her actions and no longer makes excuses. She is less impulsive and learns to abide by the company's policy and rules. She accepts that she cannot insist that things be done exactly the way she wants them. She asks her higher power through prayer and meditation to help her remove her character defects one by one.

Step 7: "Humbly asked Him to remove our shortcomings." Gayle continues to practice getting to work on time. She no longer tries to blame others for her own actions and misbehavior. Nevertheless, her deaf friends in the community expect her to remain the same person she was during her drinking days. They become resistant and confused when she tries to change her behavior. In spite of her problems, Gayle was very funny and friendly when she drank. Now that she no longer drinks, she is more of her real self, not so funny and sometimes aloof. Her deaf friends become uncomfortable, realizing that they do not really know her when she is sober. They say she is no longer fun to be with. Because of this lack of support and understanding from her deaf friends, Gayle feels less comfortable going to deaf gatherings. She attends more AA meetings in order to maintain her new sober behavior.

Step 8: "Made a list of all persons we had harmed and became willing to make amends to them all." It sometimes happens that the English word amends is translated as SORRY during interpreted AA meetings. In that case, Gayle may misunderstand the real meaning of the word as it is intended in Step 8. She must learn that it is not enough to say "I am sorry." She must also be willing to work to resolve past problems by getting to work on time, by complying with workplace policy, or paying off old financial debts to family members or friends. If she has hurt some of her deaf friends in the past, it will be difficult to make amends, even though she may see them often at deaf events such as picnics, parties, or other social gatherings. When Gayle understands the concept, she uses the sign RESOLVE to express the meaning of English word, "amends." She writes down the names of people she has hurt or disappointed, and she tries to think of a way to approach each one of them appropriately. She may even need to get help on this from her sponsor or an experienced AA friend.

Step 9: "Made direct amends to such people, wherever possible, except when to do so would injure them or others." When Gayle feels ready to make amends, she needs to discuss some strategies with her sponsor or counselor. She may make an arrangement to meet a friend she has hurt to explain her behavior and ask for forgiveness. She may pay off financial debts to some of her friends, an approach she learns about from a recovering deaf friend, Mike. Mike lived in another city during his early sober years. He shares that whenever he went back East for a deaf convention, he put aside some money in case he ran into old deaf friends. Mike was ready to pay them back even though they were no longer friends. Gayle considers this option when she thinks about how to approach deaf friends. She is afraid, though, because she feels embarrassed and humiliated about her past manipulations. She worries that gossip about her has spread far and wide to deaf people, including those who live in other parts of the country.

Step 10: "Continued to take personal inventory and when we were wrong promptly admitted it." Gayle learns that in English, "personal inventory" really means that she needs to reflect on her behavior whenever she suspects that some of her character defects are interfering with her relationships. For example, one day she gets into a heated argument with her boss. She becomes furious and walks away. Later, she calls her sponsor to talk about the incident. She feels ashamed and wrong in her behavior, but she also feels resentment because she was treated unfairly. She may go to an AA meeting and share her feelings with the group. Gayle is learning to develop accurate self-appraisal day by day. After considering the situation and the feedback of people she trusts, she tries to find a resolution. The next day she goes to her boss and apologizes for her arrogant behavior during their argument. She understands that she needs to accept that her behavior was not appropriate, no matter who is right or wrong. For Gayle, practicing Step 10 is crucial to maintaining her life with sanity and sobriety.

Step 11: "Sought through prayer and meditation to improve our conscious contact with God as we understood Him, praying only for knowledge of His will for us and the power to carry that out." Gayle learns that the goal of this Step is to develop a "relationship" with something other than herself or another human being. She remembers that in the deaf community, the ASL sign for SPIRIT is often used at deaf sporting events or other activities to indicate the strong, bonded feeling between the players. She tries to practice love and faith and to remember that "praying" or "meditating" will help her to be aware of herself and all that is happening around her. In this case, the English word "will" is translated as the sign usually meaning WANT.

To Gayle, all this is a spiritual reality. The spiritual reality is not connected to a specific religion, but it is always there for her highest good. She asks daily for the spiritual power to carry out "His will," using the ASL sign DO-IT to convey the English meaning "carry it out."

Step 12: "Having had a spiritual awakening as the result of these steps, we tried to carry this message to alcoholics and to practice these principles in all our affairs." During her work on the first 11 Steps and her study of their meaning, Gayle has tried to incorporate the lessons she was learning into her daily life and to share her success with others. She has found that the 12 Steps help her to be spiritually alert and stable. In ASL, Gayle understands the English phrase, "carry these messages" means "show examples of success in sobriety." She shares her experiences during her recovery to inform other deaf alcoholics or drug addicts and give them hope. To her a spiritual awakening means a clear understanding of the Steps. She tries to follow these Steps in all her activities at work, at home and in her social life.

Gayle accepts that working on the 12 Step program will be a lifetime process. She will need to continuously practice the 12 Steps, one day at a time and one Step at a time. She may not be able to do all these Steps for many sober years to come. The Big Book of *Alcoholics Anonymous* explains that recovering alcoholics strive for "spiritual progress", not spiritual perfection. Gayle now knows that she is does not have to be "perfect." After all, she is only human, but she is willing to "keep on keeping on" with the recovery process to the best of her ability. Now she is ready to become an example of a recovering deaf person and to share her experience, strength and hope with all other deaf and hearing friends who are struggling with their alcohol and drug problems.

An Interview with a Deaf Member of AA

The following interview with a recovering deaf alcoholic who has been in the AA program over 20 years may help further clarify some common deaf experiences with the Steps. She has agreed to answer these questions about her experiences during her recovery to the best of her knowledge, while at the same time maintaining confidentiality.

How have you benefited from the 12 Steps of Recovery?

These suggested steps are guidelines in the process of recovery, and were helpful especially during my early years of sobriety. They assisted me in making necessary changes in my life as well as changes in some of my behaviors that hindered my recovery process. Numerous changes in my life were necessary to rebuild my self esteem and improve my relationships with people, to get in touch with my higher power, and to maintain my sobriety.

What kind of assistance or guidance did you get when you were working the Steps? Did you have a sponsor? Did you use a guidebook? Did you go to Step study group meetings?

I worked through and reviewed the Steps gradually through trial and error. I got assistance by attending AA meetings, listening to knowledgeable and experienced AA members, attending Step meetings, sharing experiences with supportive AA friends before and after meetings, and working with my sponsors. However, the reality is that 90% of the effort of working through the Steps had to come from my being willing, open and honest, and doing it myself. The remaining 10% is those other things.

Betty G. Miller

What really made you get started doing the Step work?

I began the Step work when I decided to get sober. In other words, whether I knew it or not, I started with the Step work on day one of my sobriety. Step 1 was the real key to beginning the process of recovery. I could not practice the other 11 Steps or start making any changes in my life until I did Step 1 and was able to remember it daily.

Which parts of the 12 Steps were the most difficult for you?

The most difficult Steps in my early sobriety were Steps 4 and 5. I could not do them until my fourth year of sobriety. It is not that I didn't want to or that I was procrastinating. It was really a most painful process. When I first came into AA, I had no self-esteem, and I had built a thick wall around me, shutting out my feelings. I was afraid of intimacy and would not trust anyone to become close to me. It took me a long time to become honest, open, and willing — it's called H.O.W. in AA — and to work on these Steps.

I slowly developed the courage to work through these Steps with support from my sponsors and AA friends, both deaf and hearing. It was important that doing the process was without fear. I realized that I must be comfortable with Step 3, and then began start working on Step 4. I worked on Step 4 with hearing AA friends and sponsors, many who did not know Sign Language. I did my Step 5 work with my sponsors and AA friends and with Sign Language interpreters as well. This painful process required a lot of courage and effort. I have worked on these Steps again several times throughout my period of sobriety.

There are several other steps which refer to "God as We Understand Her" that I struggled with for a long time. I am not a Christian, nor am I an atheist. I believe in the Spirit that is within me, a loving and caring Woman Spirit, to keep me going in my life. I try to keep in touch with this Spirit through meditation and prayer on a daily basis, so I am prepared for when I will need to do more work on Steps 4 and 5 in later years.

Which one of the steps do you relate to most?

In maintaining my sobriety, I relate to all the Steps to support my process of recovery. I usually review the Steps, depending on what is happening with me, and the various conflicts that come up. Most of the time I refer to Step 1 (remembering that I am still a recovering alcoholic), Step 3 (letting go and trying not to control too much), and Step 10 (keeping on with my practice of the 12 Steps and principles of AA in all my affairs).

Did you work through the Steps one after the other in a chronological order? How long did it take you to work through them?

In the beginning of my sobriety, I started to work through the 12 Steps in numerical order as listed, but I stopped at Step 3. Then I would do Step 12 occasionally when newcomers needed help and support. Eventually, I become more comfortable with myself and started working through all the Steps from time to time on an ongoing basis. There are times when I refer back to different Steps such as Step 1, 3, 4, 5, 10 and 11, but not necessarily in that order. I also review the Steps 1-12 to make sure that I remember to maintain the principles.

This is a lifelong process. I see that as I have "grown up" in the stages of recovery, my understanding and perspectives have changed. I am clearer about my alcoholism than before. This is why I always consider myself a recovering alcoholic, not a recovered alcoholic.

Do you ever do Step reviews?

As I explained, I usually review the 12 Steps, choosing one or two Steps to work on, depending on what is happening with me at the time. I need to remind myself to practice the Steps in all my affairs, including personal, social and work relationships. I also know that I carry a message about my recovery through my own actions and am an example to all newcomers who wish to become sober. Above all, it is an ongoing process because if I stop doing the Steps, my old behaviors may creep back into my life. So the process of working through the 12 Steps never ends!

110 *What would be your suggestions for other people who are working the Steps?*

Don't be discouraged if you need to be sober at least one year (Step 1) before you can really understand and work through Steps 2 to Steps 12. Just keep attending meetings, including Step study groups, and listen to your AA friends, and sponsors.

Try to use ASL videotapes of the 12 Steps to assist you in understanding the 12 Steps. Read the Big Book. Listen to other recovering AA friends (deaf and hearing) who share their experiences with the Steps.

Try not to procrastinate in working through these steps, but do them when you are ready for them. To the best of your ability, stick with the first three Steps from the beginning of your sobriety. When you are ready, move on with the rest of the other Steps. Above all, get as much support and assistance as you need while working on the Steps.

Be patient with yourself in the process. (It took me almost 10 years of sobriety to gain a clear understanding of the deep meaning of the 12 Steps, all the while working slowly through the Steps).

Make changes in your lifestyle in the process of recovery using the 12 Steps as suggested guidelines (see Steps 6 and 7). Take your time. It is not easy to achieve H.O.W. (Honesty, Open-mindedness, and Willingness). Give yourself at least five years to make these changes, one day at a time.

As it is said in Chapter Five of the Big Book, "we are aiming for spiritual progress, not spiritual perfection." We are human. We do make mistakes, and we will always have setbacks in our process.

Sponsors cannot do the Steps for you. They can only be there for you to provide support and suggestions along the way.

Prepare and do the amends (Steps 8 and 9), but please do not rush to do them. When you work these Steps, get advice from your counselors or AA friends. Usually, the amends can be done long after you work through the first 7 Steps.

AA works only if you stick with the program, including the 12 Steps. Step work is a lifetime process, and it works as long as you stay clean and sober. Nobody can do it for you. 90% of the success in recovery depends on you and your honesty, open-mindedness, and willingness. The other 10% comes from the support of your AA friends and sponsors.

Work hard on H. O. W. (being honest, open-minded, and willing).

Do not be too hard on yourself. Do the best you can. Try to keep it simple and be patient with yourself. Last, but not least, stay sober!

The Twelve Traditions

The 12 Traditions apply to the AA fellowship group. They are suggested guidelines by which AA maintains its unity and relates to the "outside world." The 12 Traditions took form after a period of rapid expansion when AA was threatened by disputes over membership, money, personal relations, public relations, management of groups, clubs, and other related issues.

Over the past 20 years, it seems that deaf groups have had difficulty following some of these Traditions. The reason may be a lack of understanding of the real meaning and/or plain ignorance of the Traditions, or it may be the result of so much diversity among individual members. Many of these deaf persons come from hearing families and "mainstreamed" education programs. Because of their isolation, they did not learn to play and work with groups, except perhaps sports teams.

Use of Twelve Traditions in Deaf Meetings

The following vignettes describe some of the conflicts deaf groups experience in regard to the 12 Traditions.

Tradition 1. Our common welfare should come first: personal recovery depends on unity. The word "welfare" may have a different meaning to a deaf member, Jonathan, because of his experiences. For example, the word WELFARE as signed would probably mean social security benefits. The word COMMON may mean "we are all the same" to deaf members. Jonathan may be resistant to this, as he may feel that he is really different from the others. He will learn later that in Tradition 1 (signed GROUP RULE #1), "welfare" means the general prosperity, well being, or good of the group and that "common" means that all AA members come together to provide group support for all involved. For the common welfare to come first, this means that the members try not to think only of themselves, but also to support each other to maintain their sobriety. In other words, principles come before personalities.

Tradition 2. For our group purpose there is but one ultimate authority — a loving God as He may express Himself in our group conscience. Our leaders are but trusted servants: they do not govern. Jonathan is still uncomfortable with the words "God" and "authority," because of his past experiences. Jonathan will need time to learn that the word "God" may be just another form of describing a higher power and that the members share responsibilities for the tasks necessary to the group. Sometimes, Jonathan finds that many AA members do not have the confidence or self esteem to follow up on these responsibilities.

Tradition 3. The only requirement for AA membership is a desire to stop drinking. Jonathan does not have trouble understanding this at all, but he learns that it is an important Tradition to emphasize at the hearing AA group business meetings. It is one of the points that help clarify that the hearing AA group meetings must be accessible to all deaf members by allowing sign language interpreters in the meetings.

Tradition 4. Each group should be autonomous except in matters affecting other groups of AA as a whole. The word "autonomous" and "anonymous" or "anonymity" may look like the same English words to Jonathan. But the signs for each of these words are entirely different. He learns that this word "autonomous" really means that each AA group must support itself financially and that the group may govern itself as appropriate. He also understands that the group must follow the basic guidelines and not focus on anything that may jeopardize its purpose.

Tradition 5. Each group has but one primary purpose — to carry its message to the alcoholics who still suffer. Jonathan understands that it is essential to focus on the primary purpose of AA, and that he can only share his experience, strength and hope with other alcoholics, including deaf people, who suffer.

Tradition 6. An AA group ought never endorse, finance, or lend the AA name to any related facility or outside enterprise, lest problems of money, property, and prestige divert us from our primary purpose. Jonathan is sometimes faced with a problem in having a sign language interpreter, if the hearing group protests and uses this tradition to justify not allowing an interpreter in meetings unless he/she is in recovery. He will need to explain to the hearing members that the interpreters are being paid by outside agencies only to make the meeting accessible for Jonathan and to enable him to be with the group. Also, there is a code of ethics established for interpreters which commits them to maintaining confidentiality.

Tradition 7. Every AA group ought to be fully self-supporting, declining outside contributions. Most hearing AA groups, if large enough, are willing to donate funds from their own contributions to provide communication access for deaf members. However, if the AA group is too small, this becomes a financial and emotional problem. Even though the hearing members are supportive, they may not have sufficient funds to pay for interpreting services.

This tradition may occasionally cause a problem as it has been used by hearing members to justify excluding sign language interpreters (who are non-members) in hearing AA groups. However, over 10 years ago, the central office of AA (General Service Office), made it official that Tradition 7 does not apply to sign language interpreters who are paid by outside agencies and that hearing groups may allow non-member interpreters so as to provide access to deaf people.

Sometimes an interpreting situation occurs that may be very complex. For example, one time there was an AA Clubhouse which provided facilities and meeting space for AA members. Jonathan called the executive director of this clubhouse and asked for sign language interpreters at certain meetings. The clubhouse applied for and received funding to pay for sign language interpreters for one year, and the executive director accepted responsibility to make the arrangements. Jonathan was required to call at least one week in advance to schedule interpreters.

However, there were times, for various reasons, Jonathan did not show up at these scheduled meetings (this happens to many addicts). The director became upset and asked Jonathan to pay for these services. Then the director reprimanded Jonathan for not showing up at the meetings. This attitude discouraged Jonathan. He dropped out and did not attend these meetings after that. He saw that ongoing hearing members did not always attend meetings and did not have to inform anyone. He felt that the director was violating his rights, as well as Tradition 2 and 3. Who was right? Furthermore, the main purpose of this tradition is to avoid financial arguments that may divert from the primary purpose of AA.

Tradition 8. Alcoholics Anonymous should remain forever nonprofessional but our service centers may employ special workers. Deaf members are rarely employed as special workers to assist the AA clubhouse. Many hearing members do not know how to relate or what to do around the deaf members and may feel inadequate about not being able to communicate with them.

Tradition 9. AA, as such, should never be organized; but we may create service boards or committees directly responsible to those they serve. In AA, there are no minutes or records, except that there may be a member responsible for contributions, renting a space for meetings, and sometimes there may be a program chairperson. The members of the group usually volunteer to take care these matters. These positions usually last at least three to six months. This suggested ruling regarding service boards, for example, may be applied to an AA clubhouse, thus allowing it to apply for and received funds for interpreting services.

Tradition 10. Alcoholics Anonymous has no opinion on outside issues; hence the AA name ought never be drawn into public controversy. This includes controversies regarding deaf people, such as communication access problems that occur in local communities. Such conflicts should not be brought into the AA community.

Tradition 11. Our public relations policy is based on attraction rather than promotion; we need always maintain personal anonymity. Sometimes outside deaf organizations would like to honor a deaf member who has contributed much of his/her time in providing support to other alcoholics who suffer. As difficult as it is, it is still up to deaf members to decline such honors in order to maintain their personal anonymity.

Tradition 12. Anonymity is the spiritual foundation of all our traditions, ever reminding us to place principles before personalities. Anonymity is very important, especially to deaf members, and often difficult to maintain. For example, when Jonathan first came to the deaf AA group, he recognized another deaf member from deaf events he had attended during his drinking period. He became embarrassed and fearful because he was distrustful of this member. It may take several meetings for Jonathan to become confident that his anonymity is safe.

Jonathan also learns that anonymity actually means that it does not matter what kind of work a member does, where he/she comes from, if he/she is rich or poor, or what level education he/she has on. This includes members from the deaf communities. A member places principles above personality, and focuses on the primary purpose of AA.

Betty G. Miller

Deaf Adult Children of Alcoholics: Who are They?

The alcoholic/substance abuse family system is typically centered around the family member who is an alcoholic or drug addict. The children in this family system grow up looking at the world around them for some indication of how to behave, as well as how to feel and how to respond, rather than using their own internal process. The family is isolated, emotionally and often physically. Each member feels powerless and has very low self-esteem. They do not communicate with each other except in a crisis. For the family to continue to exist and its members to remain within this family, three rules are established. They are: don't talk, don't trust, and don't feel. (Claudia Black, 1981.)

In her presentation at the 1990 Conference on Substance Abuse and Recovery: Empowerment of Deaf Persons, Francine White, Ed.D. explained that the "don't talk" rule makes it impossible for family members to discuss the real issues behind problems such as alcoholism. The belief is that if they are ignored, they will go away. From the "don't trust" rule, children in these families learn that they are not to trust other people, and especially not to trust themselves. They feel pressure to believe the family denial instead of their own perceptions of the world. The "don't feel" rule conveys that emotions are not safe to experience or express. Since feelings are denied and repressed, these children become emotionally "numbed out." They are taught to be strong, tough, and brave in order to survive within their family system.

Deaf alcoholic parents and their children are often doubly isolated. They develop strong defenses between themselves and the rest of the world. Nevertheless, boundaries within the family system are confusing and unclear. Everyone in the family plays inappropriate roles, such as children taking care of the parents. Deaf adult children of alcoholic parents have several common experiences, such as unpredictability of events and being scapegoated for family problems. Sometimes deafness becomes an issue that diverts from the real problem or issue in the family. Unpredictable events in their home cause development of the adaptive self. They try to foresee cues that may mean trouble. For example, a father, John, comes home from work. He expects his wife, Maria, to make sure that he has a supply of beer, and for his child, Jack, to be quiet. Jack stays in his bedroom, keeping away until his father passes out. These behavior patterns may continue into adulthood, at which time the adult children may not be able to function normally and may become alcoholics or substance abusers themselves.

A deaf member of Adult Children of Alcoholics (ACOA or ACA), Judy, grew up in a deaf alcoholic family. She played the role of a "problem child" to get attention, which also drew the focus away from the underlying problem of her alcoholic mother. She even made herself a target for verbal and physical abuse. Her deaf parents isolated the family from society. Because of this, Judy, who is now in recovery, often withdraws from the deaf community. She feels the stigma of alcoholism and addiction, and feels ashamed and guilty, refusing to acknowledge or talk about her parents' addiction.

Unfortunately, the deaf community has usually been aware of the abuse of alcohol or drugs for many years, and tolerates it, whereas the "shame" of addiction is often attached to those known to be in recovery.

Recovering deaf ACOA members are often painfully ashamed of the past behavior of their parents while they were drinking or using, especially if the parents are members of the deaf community. They do not attend self-help meetings because of their shame and their denial that they have any problem themselves. Also, many deaf ACOA members in recovery refuse to go to all-deaf meetings because they feel that their confidentiality may be violated, and they do not trust the deaf people in the group to not talk about them. They cannot share their feelings. Their low self-esteem hinders their ability to express any feelings that would make them look bad. Although their behavior is not helping with their current issues, they feel that the deaf community expects them to behave in ways that are familiar.

Deaf Al-Anon Members: Who are They?

Al-Anon members are family members, significant others, and close friends who live with a recovering alcoholic/addict. The purpose of Al-Anon meetings is for these members to focus on themselves. Many of them have issues with co-dependency. Symptoms of co-dependency include "black and white thinking," blame, shame, worry, fear, poor communication, helping for the purpose of control, and feeling inadequate. These Al-Anon members care deeply and wish to protect their family. It is hard for them to let go and allow the addicted member to succeed or fail on his own. Unwittingly they may be enabling the addictive behaviors.

Many deaf family members do not attend Al-Anon meetings for two basic reasons: First, most of the deaf Al-Anon members do not understand why that they need to go to meetings. Their partner seems to be the one with the problem and there are very few interested deaf Al-Anon members with whom to share. Secondly, funding for interpreters for AA meetings usually does not extend to Al-Anon meetings.

Sometimes friends and family members expect that a quick change will happen and that the problem will go away or that the situation will improve. They may not understand the insanity of substance abuse thinking that causes an addict to repeat old behavior over and over again. Sometimes, they even think that the addict is just playing and that the behavior is funny. They do not realize that their co-dependency can be part of the problem and that they must do something different to find a solution.

Recovery can be healing for everyone involved, and meetings provide better understanding and support for all victims of the disease. The deaf community no longer needs to be feel responsible for and be protective of the deaf addict. They can learn to provide more support to recovering deaf friends and family members, and encourage them to participate in many activities to avoid isolation.

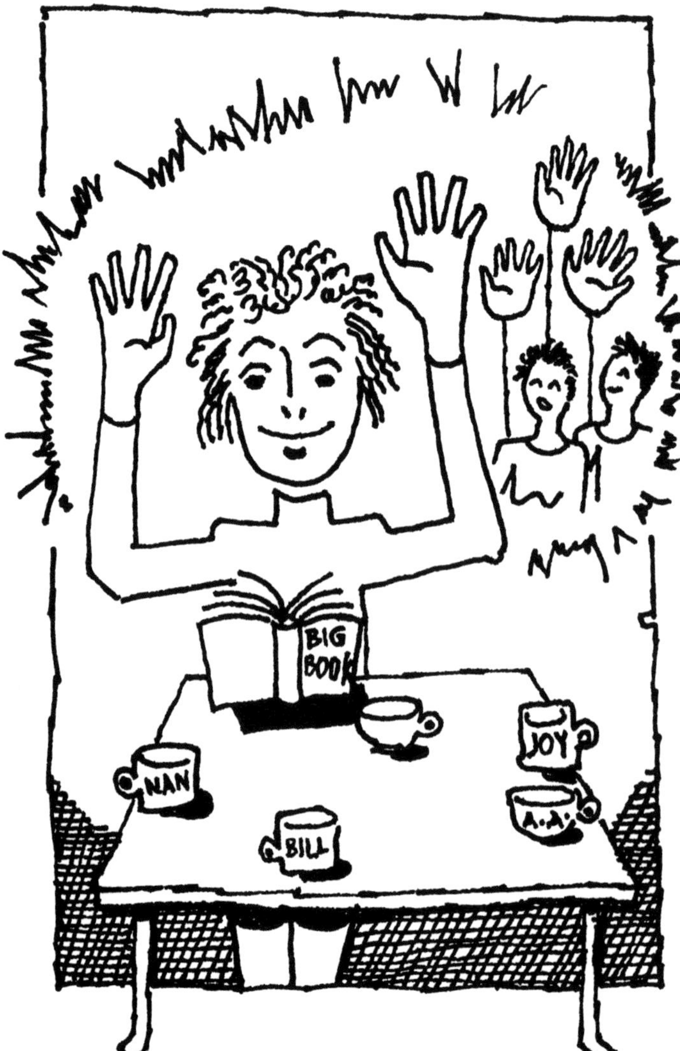
BIG BOOK
JOY
NAN
A.A.
BILL

Chapter Six

Deaf Staff in Substance Abuse Treatment Programs

Carla's Story

I have worked for three deaf treatment programs, and have had bad experiences with two of them. The first program was not practicing the principles they preached. The administration was not honest or consistent in planning for deaf patients, and sometimes set staff workers against each other. There was no policy on the use of sign language by staff members. Numbers were the main focus of the administration, and the program director seemed more concerned with image than substance. The program did not even have a clear philosophy or a mission statement.

The hearing program had a set of house and conduct rules that was different from the deaf program. The deaf patients were confused and were not sure which set of rules to follow. The deaf staff office was not even equipped with a direct phone line, so every time there was an incoming call, one of the hearing program staff had to come to the office to notify the deaf staff. This is just one example of the inequities that occurred and the administration's insensitivity to the needs of deaf staff and clients.

Although I did not feel comfortable working in this program, the recovering community in the city offered wonderful support. There were at least 20 deaf and interpreted meetings each week that I could attend. I also developed excellent contacts with both deaf and hearing recovering people which were a great asset to my ongoing recovery.

They even provided support during the difficult times that I was experiencing at the workplace.

After I left this job, I went to work at another deaf treatment program located in another state, which was also run by professionals in a clinical setting. About ninety percent of the staff was hearing with a range of sign language skills. When I arrived, I learned that the deaf program was in disarray and that the Program Director was telling everyone that I would soon whip things into shape. I didn't know I had been hired to clean things up. I thought I was hired as a counselor, with my recovery taken into account, so as to serve as a role model for the patients in the program. I soon saw that the staff lacked trust in one another, as well as the trust in the administration. Sometimes I felt concerned that some of the staff would attempt to sabotage my good standing because they felt threatened by my fluent ASL skills and my knowledge of deaf culture and by the possibility that I would move up to higher positions.

On top of the difficulties I was experiencing at this program, there were only three interpreted meetings a week that I could attend in this city. These meetings were actually meant for the patients who were in the program where I worked, but I also participated because I needed them as means of survival for my recovery.

After I resigned from this program, I moved to a job in a third deaf treatment program. This time it was a social model, which turned out to be an ideal program for someone like me who not only wanted to provide services for deaf persons in recovery, but to take part in the process of recovery as well. The program was very much like AA, with alcoholics sharing experience, strength and hope with another. The staff consisted of myself as the program director, a program assistant/interpreter, and an alcohol resource specialist. These last two positions were held by hearing persons. In addition, we relied on a volunteer staff and the program participants to maintain the program functions.

Although the program was for deaf people, quite a few recovering hearing people played a part in the program, attending meetings, hanging out, and sharing with the deaf participants. There was quite a diverse range of deaf people who took part in the program. When I left that job, there were almost 20 regular deaf participants. Presently, I am working part time and have returned to school to obtain the education I need for my future.

Why Deaf Staff?

Why is hiring culturally deaf staff in recovery programs for deaf persons important? The deaf staff may include an administrator, addiction counselor, nurse, doctor, social worker or other team worker. They seem to enhance the recovery process for deaf patients for the following reasons:

1) They provide effective language and role models for participants, families, friends, and hearing staff.

2) They ensure that effective communication will happen at least some of the time.

3) They decrease the likelihood that deafness, per se, is pathologized.

4) Their presence limits the use of deafness as a defense — "if you were deaf, you'd understand" — and helps participants feel safe enough to respond to treatment.

5) They give a program credibility in the deaf community which, in turn, increases referrals and promotes recruitment of additional deaf staff.

6) They sensitize the hospital/agency to the abilities as well as the needs of deaf participants.

7) Their presence makes hearing staff feel the work environment is exciting and special, thus decreasing staff turnover.

8) They insure that a culturally deaf viewpoint is at least factored into every decision affecting deaf patients.

Staff Issues

Sometimes, a deaf professional may leave his career as a counselor because his need to help other deaf people decreases, or because after several years of sobriety, a deaf program manager may discover that she is in the wrong job and pursue a career change. However, it is far more common for deaf caregivers to leave the field because of personal and interpersonal conflicts that could be avoided. This chapter deals with deaf and hearing staff who work together in substance abuse treatment programs. There are several issues to be considered: 1) co-dependency and enabling is a common problem for both deaf and hearing staff; 2) communication and cultural differences require flexibility and education; 3) stress and feelings of alienation may lead to burn-out for deaf staff.

Co-Dependency and Enabling

Anne Wilson Schaef in her book, *Co-Dependence, Misunderstood — Mistreated,* offers the following description of co-dependency: "Co-dependence is a disease that has many forms and expressions and that grows out of a disease process that is inherent in the system in which we live." She also quotes Robert Subby who has defined co-dependence as "an emotional, psychological, and behavioral condition that develops as a result of an individual's prolonged exposure to, and practice of, a set of oppressive rules: rules which prevent the open expression of feeling as well as the direct discussion of personal and interpersonal problems."

Basically, co-dependency means that an individual focuses on another person's feelings and behavior more than on his or her own. This individual allows the other's actions, reactions, successes and failures to dominate her life, her energy, and her attention. She neglects her own wants, needs and feelings to spend her time defining, second guessing or attempting to control another person. A colleague at a substance abuse conference shared with me this humorous definition of co-dependency with a terrific hidden message: When Brian was near the end of a long illness and in the process of dying, he had flashbacks of his life from childhood to the present. But when a co-dependent woman, Jennifer, was close to death, she experienced flashbacks of her spouse's life instead of her own. Co-dependence is common in dysfunctional families.

The dictionary definition of "enabling" is "to help" or "empower." In the language of recovery, however, "to enable" means to hinder the healing process. Enabling involves the unintentional encouragement of behavior patterns that grow out of the disease of co-dependence. Sometimes therapists and other professionals or caregivers in the substance abuse field are unaware of their own co-dependence and unintentionally participate in perpetuating the abuse. In other words, those who are helpers, trapped in the denial of their own disease, are making their clients worse by enabling the client's sick behavior. This can easily happen to both hearing and deaf professionals who work with deaf people, but certain cultural norms make this a serious issue for deaf staff.

Co-Dependency and the Deaf Community

The deaf community is relatively small, close, and has high expectations of conformity. As in the hearing world, many deaf people have become transient, moving from one city or state to another because of their jobs and careers. They maintain contact with each other through deaf sports tournaments, conventions, and sometimes through electronic mail and faxes, as well as the TTY. Deaf leaders from deaf clubs, organizations, and associations coordinate activities for deaf people who often participate in groups, discuss matters as a group and arrive at a group consensus. The deaf leaders may ask for volunteers to work with them on certain projects, but it is often difficult to find volunteers for political or advocacy work or other services. Most people prefer to work on social activities like picnics. The deaf members have co-dependent relationships with their leaders. And the leaders themselves often accept and enable these behaviors.

Most deaf people who participate in deaf clubs have no desire to attain a leadership position. One possible reason is they have low self-esteem and a great fear of failing or being criticized for their mistakes. Deaf leaders are willing to take responsibility for the success or failure of group events. If there is a problem, deaf people do not confront each other directly. Instead they talk to friends about a leader's actions or behavior, with the expectation that friends will pass the information along. This is accepted process and is referred to in the deaf community as deaf gossip. This is one way that co-dependency operates in the community.

Dave

Dave, a well known deaf leader who is in recovery, shares that he recognizes his co-dependent behavior. He is currently employed as a counselor for a treatment program, working with deaf and hard of hearing patients. He is also a well-known leader at the deaf club, and takes full responsibility for all activities that take place at the club.

One day, he was offered a new job that would have required him to move away from the city. It was a higher paying job with more responsibility, and he was looking forward to moving ahead with his counseling career. However, after talking about this with deaf friends, some of the club members approached him with their fears that the club would fall apart if he left. Feeling upset and guilty, he then decided to refuse the job and stay in the city. Today, he regrets this decision, but, at the same time, he accepts responsibility for his actions and recognizes that he encouraged and enabled this dependent behavior. He also realizes that stress from this co-dependent behavior is straining his own recovery process. He knows he must learn to balance community values and his own personal needs.

Some recovering deaf people make the choice to maintain a low profile and stabilize their sobriety before they return to deaf community activities. They often tend to wait until they have learned new ways to handle stress and have confronted some of their own personal issues. A few recovering deaf people become more involved and are able to work successfully in substance abuse treatment programs, but most, especially newly recovering deaf staff, find themselves encouraging and enabling others or risking their own sobriety.

A deaf professional may also have experienced and learned dysfunctional behavior from co-dependent professional helpers who were their teachers, houseparents, and school counselors. For example, when Brian was young, a school counselor encouraged him to change his behavior to fit into the hearing world. Now a professional himself, Brian occasionally falls back on what he learned through past experience and takes a similar approach to his work with deaf people.

Dual Relationships

In *Issues and Ethics in the Helping Professions* by Corey, Corey, and Callanan, the authors note that "...there has been an increasing concern over dual relationships as an ethical issue," and point to growing professional literature that offers various perspectives on this issue. What is a dual relationship, and how does this apply to deaf people and their relationships with clients? "Dual relationships occur when counselors blend their professional relationship with a client with another kind of relationship. Dual relationships, which can take many forms, have been called a violation of ethical, legal, and clinical standards." (Pope, 1984.)

Because the deaf community is so small and the needs so specific, this may create special problems for deaf professionals. For instance, a deaf counselor, Judith, who is in recovery herself, needs interpreters for AA meetings. She may meet some of her clients at these meetings, and her position may become ambiguous. Is she is there for her own recovery or to act as a sponsor/mentor and provide support to the other deaf members? With so few interpreted meetings in the area, where can this deaf therapist can go without running into a deaf AA member who may be a client? Likewise, a deaf therapist may not be able to attend all-deaf meetings and remain anonymous. There are no special meetings for deaf professional caregivers who are in recovery. Attending events sponsored by deaf clubs and organizations, deaf counselors inevitably come into contact with deaf clients who socialize in the same circle. Often when deaf professionals meet with a deaf client seeking assistance, they find out that it is a friend of a friend or someone they know from the past.

Deaf therapists may also become too involved with their clients because of their own unresolved deaf issues. They may feel they need to prove themselves and try to control the client's wants, feelings, and needs. Deaf or hearing professionals may become paternalistic and attempt to make decisions for their clients based on their own assumptions, second-guessing what is best for these clients.

Other dual relationship examples, as described by Keith-Spiegel and Koocher (1985), are combining roles of teacher and therapist, bartering therapy for goods or services, providing therapy to a relative or a friend's relative, socializing outside therapy sessions, and becoming emotionally or sexually involved with a client or former client. "A key question is: Whose needs are being met, the therapist's or the client's? To us, behavior is unethical when it reflects a lack of awareness or concern about the impact of the behavior on clients. Therapists who engage in more than one role with clients may be trying to meet their own financial, social, or emotional needs." (Corey, Corey, and Callanan, p. 141.)

What about culturally appropriate behaviors in the deaf community and their impact on the relationship between the deaf therapist and client? Often, the therapist will need support to face the on-going challenges and the need to constantly reassess and set appropriate boundaries. After the deaf participants complete their treatment, they will go back to their own homes and re-enter the deaf community. Most of the deaf and hearing staff have little or no contact with the deaf community in which their clients interact, except occasionally on a professional level. They may continue counseling with these recovering deaf people on a weekly basis during aftercare. In a session with a deaf counselor, however, the deaf client will usually begin by discussing the "deaf news" of the community. A client may disclose that other recovering participants have relapsed, drinking or using or both. The deaf therapist must find ways to avoid such information without offense, bending but not breaking the cultural "rules" that are normally followed in the deaf community.

It is crucial that an addictive deaf therapist is fully aware of basic ethical practice, as well as her own limits and values. Consultation and support from colleagues may be valuable and necessary to assist the therapist. She can attend Al-Anon meetings, which may also help in dealing with this situation. The therapist, if at all possible, should avoid seeing her deaf clients at any events she knows they are attending. Such avoidance takes practice, but it can be successful.

Bill

Bill, a deaf addiction counselor, attends meetings at the deaf group. He has been in recovery from alcohol/drug abuse and has maintained his sobriety for seven years. He works for a non-profit agency as a counselor for deaf persons with alcohol and drug abuse problems. The deaf members from the deaf AA group look up to Bill as their role model. Bill is generous and supportive to all members of the deaf group. He is fully aware of the possible co-dependent behaviors that may occur between the deaf members and himself and he tries to avoid them.

He helps the members of the deaf AA group by attending meetings, providing education about 12 Steps, taking responsibilities for some extra activities for the deaf members, and giving rides to some of them who can not afford transportation to attend these meetings. They all look up to him to resolve some of their problems.

One day, Bill decides on a career change and goes back to school to pursue his new dream. Later, Bill finds an excellent, challenging position. He buys a new home and starts to develop new friendships. Meanwhile, he keeps in touch with Joanne, who is one of the deaf members from the old group. Joanne shares that some deaf AA members blame Bill for their relapses. They are angry at him for leaving them. Bill is saddened by this, but he also recognizes and understands their feelings. He does not feel hurt because he recognizes the co-dependent tendencies and understands that their feelings are not really about him.

Co-dependency and Hearing Staff

In a drug/alcohol treatment setting, a hearing therapist counseling a hearing client will be able to pick up on conversational styles, innuendoes, tone of voice and other nonverbal behavioral cues, and use that information as part of the counseling. With a deaf client, a hearing therapist, especially one who has little or no contact with the deaf community, may not have access to these cues. If the therapist and the deaf client are communicating through an interpreter, the interpreter may not be able to "read" such information, or may not be able to express some of the subtleties. The interpreter also may fail to convey important information to the therapist due to a lack of knowledge or training about the counseling process. Often the cues will be construed differently by a deaf person than by a hearing person. This may unintentionally cause misunderstanding, and the therapist may unwittingly encourage some unacceptable behaviors

Many deaf clients, such as Derek, a deaf addict, will tell hearing therapists, "The deaf community is small. I must maintain anonymity. I don't want to go to deaf meetings or meetings that already have interpreters. I don't want other deaf people to know." An enabling, hearing therapist, who has no background in deafness and Deaf culture, may take this message at face value and support him. However, it is possible that Derek is using truths about the deaf community as a way to avoid recovery, rather than expressing legitimate concern. Lack of knowledge on the part of the therapist may lead to enabling the deaf client.

Sometimes deaf clients behave differently with hearing therapists than they do with deaf therapists or other deaf people. They may have internalized the concept that hearing people are better than deaf people, have more knowledge and education, and therefore know more. With this concept deeply embedded in their subconscious, deaf clients will often behave with hearing therapists in a way that they think will win the counselor's approval, not the way they do when they are being themselves with other members of the deaf community.

Because of these differences in behavior, the hearing therapist may think that therapy is going well, but only because it is going the way the therapist expects it. Actually, the deaf client is not improving in any substantial way. This is a common problem that causes disagreements between hearing and deaf staff during staff meetings and results in very different evaluations on the progress report of the same deaf participant.

Sometimes the hearing therapist or the interpreter has not confronted their unconscious prejudices regarding deafness, Deaf culture, and related topics. They may have biased ideas and attitudes about deaf people that impede their work or inadvertently convey such an impression. To deaf people, the position of certain signs may indicate an condescending attitude. For example, the sign "counseling" or "helping" is normally positioned at the level of the signer's chest. If the counselor signs this word while moving in a subtly downwards direction, it may indicate that he subconsciously places himself/herself above the client. Finally, some deaf and hearing staff persons may be adult children of alcoholic adults with their own unresolved issues.

Involving a Third Party (a Sign Language Interpreter) in Therapy

As mentioned earlier, even a certified interpreter may have difficulty picking up on subtle cues in the communication process and conveying them. Furthermore, the interpreter may not have knowledge of how counseling works and the kinds of information the therapist needs.

In the revised edition (1990) of *Interpreting: An Introduction* by Nancy Frishberg, there is a discussion about therapy and counseling.

She describes some common problems that arise over time between the therapist, client and interpreter in treatment:

> The therapist may feel intruded upon on his or her own turf, may be uncertain of how to behave with a deaf person (where to look, how to address the client), and may feel left out or that rapport is difficult to gain. The client may be unfamiliar with therapy and may bring feelings from past interpreted encounters to the therapy sessions. The issue of trust in relation to confidentiality and accuracy in translation is likely to be a live one for the client. The interpreter may feel put in an awkward position: on the one hand, the interpreter may have some understanding of deafness that the therapist does not, but may feel it is beyond the role to take the initiative to explain that understanding…

While the therapist is watching the deaf person's facial expressions, the interpreter will try to convey through tone of voice what those expressions mean. What both of these people may misunderstand is that many deaf facial expressions are linguistic — having to do with syntax and grammar — rather than emotional indicators as a hearing person's facial expressions would be, and which are probably more familiar to the therapist.

Conflicts Between Deaf and Hearing Staff

Communication breakdowns are common when there are both deaf and hearing staff. Usually there are a majority of hearing people on the staff. Even with the best of intentions, the deaf staff often miss out on essential information. For example, the hearing people may try to use sign language and spoken English simultaneously to include everyone in the conversation, but it is impossible to communicate in two languages at the same time. Very often their signing will drop off and become smaller and intermittent while they continue talking. Furthermore there are nuances and idioms that do not translate well from one language to the other. This can cause considerable confusion to the deaf staff, especially when the hearing staff is not aware there are cultural differences. Of course, deaf staff may also share information about the program, policy, and other issues with each other and fail to pass the information along, creating still another possibility for conflict.

Lack of specific programming to provide hearing staff with essential information about deaf issues, Deaf culture, and ASL may contribute to conflict between deaf and hearing co-workers. Deaf staff also may lack access to "hearing culture," but because of their minority status, most deaf people have had to make adjustments to hearing culture all their lives. This imbalance may create negative feelings among the hearing staff. Deaf and hearing staff members may disagree on some behavior issues and treatment techniques in working with deaf clients. Hearing staff may feel threatened by a deaf staff worker's ability to relate directly with deaf clients. They may feel incompetent and inadequate. The differences in perspective, communication breakdowns, and cultural misunderstandings sometimes cause division and alienation among the deaf and hearing staff members. This may impact the quality of treatment and cause confusion among deaf clients. The clients may lose confidence if they sense a lack of trust among the staff.

There are several ways that this scenario generally plays itself out. For example, a typical deaf program is set up specifically for the "hearing impaired" and staffed with both hearing and deaf therapists. The term "hearing impaired" is not acceptable to many deaf people, including deaf staff, because it connotes the idea that they are "broken" hearing people instead of addressing more profound linguistic and cultural differences. Deaf staff may take issue with the (usually hearing) management of the treatment program about the label, but management often continues to use the phrase either because they do not accept the argument's validity or for political reasons. For example, management may feel that "hearing impaired" is the most effective term to use in proposals requesting funding. When the deaf clients become aware of this dispute, they are put in the awkward position of making judgments about who is right or wrong. They may feel that deaf staff are not respected or that their views are not valid. This divisiveness fosters confusion and animosity that is detrimental to recovery.

Burnout

Another scenario occurs in mainstream programs. There may be only one deaf staff member to work with the deaf clients in a mostly hearing environment. The program has a limited budget for treatment, so the director does not provide a sign language interpreter except when there are staff meetings, nor is there any training for the hearing majority who may have insufficient knowledge about deafness, Deaf culture, and related issues. It is easy to become overwhelmed or burned out with work when important staff training needs have low priority. The hearing majority staff team will be making decisions that affect the deaf clients and deaf staff without any true understanding of the basic needs of deaf people.

Sometimes a treatment program hires a deaf counselor with an expectation that because the counselor is in recovery, she will not only work with the deaf clients, but will also become a good role model to both the deaf clients and hearing staff members. Yet at the same time, the hearing staff may question the deaf person's credibility, and may even sabotage that person's reputation and opportunities for career advancement. This kind of political power struggle may be a result of mismanagement on the part of the administration.

Peter

Peter was hired as a deaf counselor in a mainstreamed program that included deaf participants. When he started, he felt uncomfortable because he sensed that some of the hearing staff were wary and holding back. Later, he learned that the program manager had told the staff that he expected Peter to mediate many of the conflicts in the program. It was Peter's understanding that he was to use his counselling skills, his fluent ASL, and his knowledge of deaf culture and community to work individually with deaf clients. He did not want to be responsible for staff relations, especially since when he did offer a suggestion, it was usually ignored. The misunderstandings and differences in perspective between Peter, the other counselors, and the administration became so severe that he decided to leave the position after only a few months.

In some mainstreamed treatment programs the hearing staff look forward to working with and learning from deaf staff members. In the beginning, there are usually positive and sincere feelings and a strong sense of commitment with good intentions. Yet, the reality is that when a deaf staff member remains in the program for a long period, a breakdown of relations between the deaf and hearing staff may occur. Instead of cancelling a meeting when there is no interpreter available, hearing staff members may attempt to sign to the deaf staff; however, not being fluent, they usually leave out important information.

In the beginning, hearing staff often ask the deaf staff members to teach them sign language, but because of the staff's heavy workload and because it is difficult to learn a new language as an adult, there may be a declining interest to pursue serious study after a few basics like greetings and fingerspelling. The deaf staff members become more isolated as time goes by, as they are often left out of the normal flow of conversation and information exchange outside of staff meetings. Feelings of guilt and shame among the staff lead to a cycle of alienation, co-dependency, avoidance, resentment, and anger.

In another scenario, deaf workers may have already internalized co-dependent character traits that they picked up in deaf clubs or organizations. These traits, if not recognized or identified, can create negative feelings, lower self-esteem, and lead to burnout. In deaf AA meetings, deaf "leaders," no matter how long they have been sober, are supposed to be role models and are expected to assist and tend to the needs of others. (In AA, there is not supposed to be any leader in the group except for a secretary, program chairperson, and a treasurer. In deaf groups, the deaf members usually regard a deaf member who has been sober a long time as a "leader.") If a deaf "leader" makes a mistake or does something that the members do not like or think is inappropriate, they may gossip among themselves. They do not confront him/her to discuss the behavior. Many "leaders" leave the deaf AA group rather than continue to struggle and ward off personal attacks in the recovering deaf community. Instead they seek out hearing meetings that no other deaf AA members attend.

Marybeth

A similar problem occurs when Marybeth, a deaf addiction counselor, relocates to accept a job in a new city. She faces not only the normal stresses of relocation, but additional problems because of being deaf. Generally, when someone moves to a new city, he or she will begin looking for new friends among their co-workers. For Marybeth, a new job feels more like moving to a foreign country because the co-workers she sees everyday do not speak the same language or belong to the same culture. She attempts to seeks out other deaf people in the city for friendship and support, but because her job is demanding, she does not have a lot of time. Furthermore, deaf people, who are busy with work and family and who live in different parts of town, find it difficult to incorporate a new deaf person into their lives. Sometimes it takes a deaf newcomer as long as two or three years to become comfortably situated in a new deaf community.

Marybeth is in recovery, and she needs to find AA support. Most of the recovering deaf people that she comes in contact with are participating in the program where she is working. Marybeth wants to meet deaf people in the city who are in recovery, but who are not connected to her work in the treatment program. Attending the same self-help meetings as her deaf clients can create a conflict of interest for Marybeth and prevent her from getting support for her own needs. To avoid this conflict, she sometimes searches for hearing self-help meetings and brings a sign language interpreter, if she can find one who does not interpret at her workplace.

Interpreters for Deaf Staff

In smaller cities, problems arise because of the limited number of interpreters. For example, the interpreter for Peter's meetings was a recovering person herself who often worked alongside Peter at the treatment program. Peter wanted to bring up his problems at work during the meetings, but he did not want to share this information with the interpreter. Peter was put in the position of needing to make a decision between his recovery needs and his needs for confidentiality. He only felt comfortable discussing his problems at work with a few co-workers and friends, excluding the interpreter.

Having staff interpreters will significantly improve communication on the job; however, it may slow down the recovery process for deaf staff members because sign language interpreters often attend events in the deaf community. Deaf caregivers often do not want to mix their social life with their personal problems or situations at work. This area and other interpreting issues will be discussed more in Chapter 7.

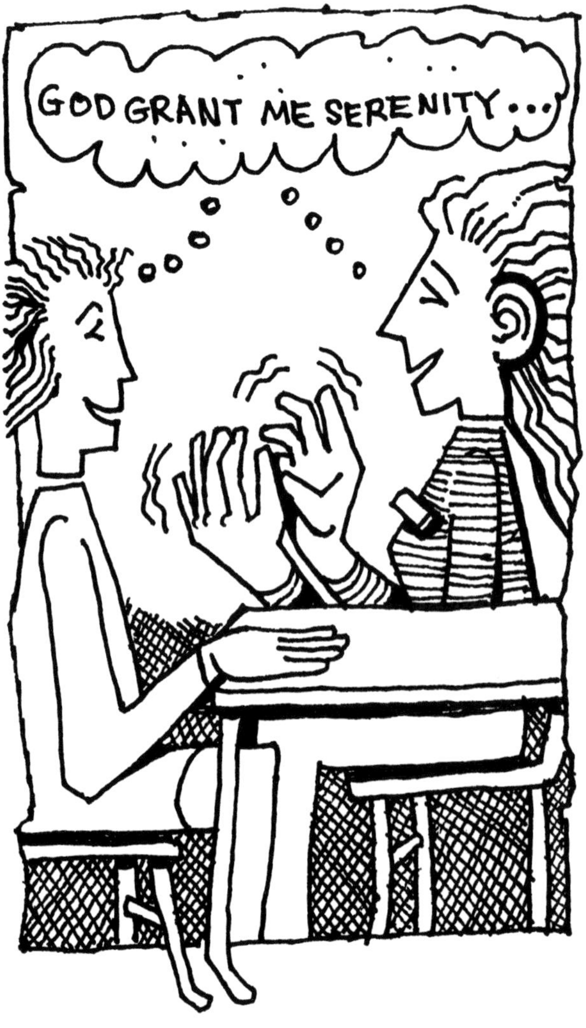
GOD GRANT ME SERENITY...

Chapter Seven

Interpreting Issues

Jennifer's Story

After completing an inpatient program, I arrive home with many concerns about whether or not I will be successful in staying sober. I know that I need to attend AA/NA meetings, find an AA/NA sponsor, and continue to work with an addiction counselor. I cannot hang out with my old friends who still use and drink heavily. I must try to find new friends.

I live in a small town where there are not many deaf people. The hearing members of AA/NA groups in this area are not used to being around deaf people or having a sign language interpreter attend their meetings. I do the best I can to explain how the interpreter will sign and voice so that the hearing members and I can share our experience, strength and hope. The hearing AA members are receptive to this, but sometimes I feel a "wall" between the hearing AA/NA members and me because we do not communicate directly to each other: there is always be a third party between us.

I called an agency for the deaf and asked for a sign language interpreter for AA meetings. The agency can only provide interpreting services for AA meetings twice a week. Making arrangements for interpreting services takes so much time and effort. Sometimes it is all I can think or worry about until the interpreter is confirmed. Even when the agency finds an interpreter for a meeting, this interpreter may not want to interpret meetings on a regular basis. They may be willing to work only the first meeting or two. I feel frustrated and sometimes cannot find another interpreter to accept the job, so I cannot continue with these meetings. Sometimes I have contacted one of my close friends for help. She and I grew up together. She is a certified interpreter. She has offered to interpret on a regular basis at the AA meetings, but I have mixed feelings. I feel relieved that I can have clear communication on a regular basis, but, at the same time, she is close to me as a friend. There are some personal things I feel I cannot share at the meetings when she is there.

Some people call themselves interpreters and are available for these meetings. The hearing people think these interpreters are truly skilled, but they are not. They are unable to read some of my signs and my fingerspelling. I have to repeat myself a few times before they understand me and that often upsets my train of thought. Nevertheless, they seem to think that they are doing well. What can I do about this? Call the agencies and explain my concerns? What if the agencies cannot find better qualified interpreters? This puts me in a dilemma — if I ask for better qualified interpreters, I may end up with no interpreted meetings to attend. Maybe it is better for me to keep quiet and to tolerate interpreters whose skills are "good enough" or "better than nothing."

Julie: A Hearing AA Member's Story

Julie is a five year member of AA, and she is hearing. She attends three or four meetings a week. It has been her experience that a lot of interaction between AA members, such as individually sharing personal experiences and problems, goes on after the official AA meeting. This interaction can be one of the most important parts of AA. It is after the meetings that the members offer very specific advice, support and understanding that may not be shared during meetings. In the interpreted meetings that Julie attends, the hearing AA members have become accustomed to the interpreter's presence. Some of them try to communicate through an interpreter with deaf members prior to or after the meeting. This is limited because most interpreters either arrive on time or late for meetings and usually leave immediately afterwards. As a result, Julie notices that it may be hard for deaf newcomers, but she is not sure how to help them feel welcome and part of the AA fellowship.

Most AA newcomers tend to wait for people to come to them. However, hearing people who have never been in contact with deaf people often feel a certain amount of awkwardness, shyness, or fear. If a brand new deaf person comes in, how can a hearing member with no signing skill offer friendship? These questions constantly trouble hearing members of AA. Many of these hearing members feel inadequate. They fear appearing paternalistic, or they wonder if they are being ignored. They do not know how to use the sign language interpreter to interact with the deaf members. Communication is an essential tool for most people in recovery. Discomfort over how to communicate with deaf people can cause feelings of alienation or deliberate avoidance. As a result, intentionally or not, the deaf person feels isolated in the midst of all the sharing at a meeting.

These two stories are typical of incidents that occur among recovering deaf and hearing people who attend interpreted meetings. Before we go on, we need to look at the common interpreting issues that occur at the alcohol/drug abuse treatment programs, and the AA/NA meeting settings.

The Interpreter's Role

The role of an interpreter in any setting is to transmit messages from the user of one language to the user of another language. A good interpreter must not only transmit the words of the language, but must also interpret the "meta-language," which includes a sense of the underlying meanings and context. Skilled interpreters are sensitive to cultural issues, respect deaf people and have a positive attitude about deaf and hearing people.

A good interpreter must also be able to adapt to the linguistic needs of the deaf people involved. Because of the variety of educational methods and sign language systems used in educational programs, not all deaf people are completely exposed to American Sign Language during their youth. Sometimes, an interpreter who has studied ASL as a second language may be better educated about the grammatical structure of ASL than some deaf people. Interpreters, however, must be able to vary their linguistic knowledge to match the linguistic skill of the deaf person. Sometimes the interpreter may use a kind of signed pidgin, made up of ASL and other sign modes.

In ordinary usage, the terms "interpretation," "transliteration" and "translation" might be considered synonyms for one another. Among the people working in these fields, they refer to quite different processes. Strictly speaking, *interpretation* refers to the process of changing messages produced in one language immediately into another language. The languages in question may be spoken or signed, but the defining characteristic is the live and immediate transmission of one distinct language to another.

Transliteration refers to the live and immediate transmission of one language into another mode of the same language, such as transliterating spoken English into one of the varieties of signed English that have been developed in the past fifty years. Some of these "codes" for English break the rules of ASL and are difficult for deaf people to understand. *Translation* implies interpretation without the additional pressure of time, such as translating a videotaped ASL speech into a written form for presentation at a later date.

Some of the most popular interpreters were raised in families where either their mother, their father, or both, are deaf. Many of these interpreters are referred to as Children of Deaf Adults (coda), after an organization of the same name (but referred to with all caps: CODA). Many of these codas grew up with ASL as their first language, and some have gone on to graduate from formal training programs where they studied the linguistics of ASL and English and developed their interpreting skills. Not all codas are good interpreters, and not all know how to sign. However, those who do enter the interpreting field are often preferred by some deaf people who value their familiarity with Deaf culture as much as their signing skills in ASL.

Selecting a Certified Interpreter

Although it is not an absolute guarantee, the best assurance of an interpreter's skills is to make sure that she/he has been certified by a qualified national entity, such as the National Association of the Deaf (NAD) or the Registry of Interpreters for the Deaf (RID).

A certified interpreter usually goes through several years of training, first in sign language including deaf culture and linguistics, and then in interpreting. Interpreters who hold valid NAD or RID certification are generally able to interpret spoken English into ASL and likewise render ASL into spoken English.

Qualified interpreters may be screened for advanced Legal certification through RID. There is, however, no other specialized certification available for the medical/mental health fields or substance abuse treatment programs which include individual and group counseling, educational classes prayer groups, and AA/NA meetings.

NAD Levels III, IV, and V certification means that holders have demonstrated competence in both interpretation and transliteration, and are recommended for a broad range of work assignments.

RID CI and CT certification (interpretation and transliteration, respectively) means that holders have demonstrated competence in both interpretation and transliteration, and are recommended for a broad range of work assignments. Both certificates together replace the previous Comprehensive Skills Certificate (CSC), which was offered until 1987.

The NAD and the RID (NAD-RID Task Force on Interpreting) are working toward development of a new system for national interpreter certification as well as compilation of "best practices" in the area of interpreting.

Betty G. Miller

Code of Ethics

Certified interpreters are expected to follow a code of ethics. For example, the interpreter who interprets for a hearing addiction counselor and a recovering deaf client is bound by both the NAD and RID Code of Ethics not to reveal to anyone what was discussed or done during the session. In fact, interpreters may not discuss their jobs with anyone unless the job is performed in public. This means that an interpreter who is working on the platform next to the mayor may repeat the mayor's comments to friends who did not attend the speech, but may not repeat or discuss comments the mayor made offstage to a deaf person in a private discussion.

The interpreter, when discussing general work experiences with friends or others, must not reveal any identifying characteristics of the individuals involved — this is especially important with members of the deaf community who know each other well. Sometimes an interpreter thinks she or he is being discreet when discussing a job, yet provides enough clues for the deaf people they are talking with to guess who they are talking about. It is best, therefore, that interpreters refrain from discussing their interpreting jobs with anyone.

Confidentiality

One point to be aware of about confidentiality is that the courts do not recognize the binding nature of the interpreter's code of ethics. An interpreter will sometimes be called into court to testify about a work situation. Unless the interpreter was working within a situation of confidentiality that the court does recognize, such as an interview between a lawyer and her deaf client or between a doctor and his deaf patient, the judge may order the interpreter to either break the code of ethics or face charges of contempt of court.

The law makes a distinction between certified and qualified interpreters. A certified interpreter may not always be a qualified interpreter for a specific deaf person. Sometimes a deaf person has been raised in an isolated deaf community or within a minority culture that uses its own sign language. Perhaps the deaf person was raised with only "home signs," the set of signs and gestures made up within a family to communicate with each other. In those situations, the certified interpreter may not be able to provide accurate interpretation. In these cases, the qualified interpreter may be a family member or a deaf member of the same community who also knows standard ASL. This individual will function as a relay interpreter between the client and the hearing, certified interpreter. RID provides certification for deaf relay interpreters, called the Certified Deaf Interpreter (CDI) certification. Deaf interpreters often provide services in legal settings.

Service providers who hire interpreters for their deaf clients need to be aware of these distinctions so that they can make a proper assessment of the situation and hire certified and qualified interpreters to meet the needs of the provider and the deaf client. It is also important to note that family members often do not possess adequate sign language skills to effectively interpret in a substance abuse treatment setting. Even if family members or friends are fluent in sign language, they are often too emotionally or personally involved to interpret effectively, accurately, and impartially. Furthermore, issues of patient confidentiality invariably arise and cause problems when family members and friends act as interpreters. This general discussion only touches the surface of interpreting issues in recovery. There are many other interpreting issues that may come up during recovery.

Interpreting Issues in Treatment and AA Settings

1) Interpreters may be regarded by newly recovering deaf AA members as power figures. They trust the interpreter to voice accurately whatever the deaf person is sharing without evaluating their skills and even allow the interpreter to speak for them about certain issues related to Deaf culture and deaf people.

Betty G. Miller

2) Some deaf members use interpreters as barriers to avoid the challenge of developing relationships with hearing AA hearing members at the meetings.
3) Co-dependency may be a problem for both sign language interpreters and recovering deaf persons.
4) Neither deaf nor hearing AA members may know how to work with interpreters. They may need to be educated about their mutual responsibilities. In some cases, hearing members may approach interpreters with questions on deafness and related topics and not talk with deaf members at all.
5) Some interpreters have the linguistic skills, but are not emotionally prepared for the intensity of AA meetings.
6) Who decides on the kind of sign language to be used (ASL, signed English, or other modes)? Sometimes hearing AA/NA members who learn a little about sign language try to participate in making this decision, ignoring the deaf members' judgement.
7) Some deaf members are not consistent in attending interpreted meetings. They may attend two meetings in a row, and then miss a meeting the following week.
8) Some interpreters do not understand the 12 Steps and 12 Traditions and slogans, and are unable to translate them appropriately for deaf members.
9) Should interpreters who are in recovery themselves interpret at AA/NA meetings?^
10) Who should interpreters ask for feedback to evaluate their skills?
11) Interpreters may arrive late or not show up at all.
12) To whom and how should deaf members complain about the interpreter's skills or behavior?
13) Who is responsible for funding for sign language interpreters at AA/NA meetings?

14) Who is responsible for the proper seating arrangements for interpreters and the deaf members?
15) What are the risks involving confidentiality and the interpreter's Code of Ethics?

Interpreting Issues in Treatment Programs

Power is one of several recurring issues that complicates the role of interpreters in treatment programs. An interpreter can become the pivotal figure in a deaf person's recovery because both the deaf patient and the hearing counselor must depend on this third party for communication. Both the hearing and the deaf person must be able to trust the interpreter's skills in English and ASL. How accurately the interpreter voices for the deaf client can be a deciding factor in a counselor's decisions about treatment, and conversely, how well the interpreter conveys the meaning and attitude of the counselor can make all the difference in the deaf person's chance for successful recovery.

In an ideal interpreting situation between a hearing counselor and a deaf client, the interpreter is aware of the many differences between hearing/deaf language and culture and is able to translate these large and small differences while he/she is interpreting. For example, in the deaf signing culture, the idiom "if you don't mind" requires a "yes" answer, with the understanding that "can you" or "are you able" is the true meaning of the question. In hearing culture, the phrase, "if you don't mind, involves a "no" answer, meaning "no, I don't mind" Ideally, if the counselor asks a "don't mind" question and the deaf client has signed "yes", the interpreter would voice "no, I don't mind," thereby satisfying both the counselor and the client's expectations in the exchange.

If, as is often the case, the interpreter is not aware of these issues, then the communication falls apart because of the misrepresentation of feelings. This places the burden of understanding and resolving these issues on the counselor and the client. In this case, the counselor may become confused because the client has said that he is unwilling to do what was requested. The counselor may repeat the request. The client may become upset that he is being asked again or angry that he is not being understood. This anger, in turn, would be misunderstood by the counselor, who may then decide that the client is uncooperative. No one realizes that a misinterpretation is at the root of this conflict.

The interpreter's behavior may also have a strong effect on the client's experience in the hearing treatment program. An interpreter who shows up late, for example, has already set up a situation of mistrust and anger. Both counselor and client are angry and frustrated by the lack of communication and the waste of their valuable time. This is tripled if the interpreter doesn't show up at all. When this kind of thing happens, the counselor may be inclined to give up on the client, or the client may decide to leave the treatment program as frustration builds up.

Similarly, most mainstream programs are unprepared for emergency situations. They do not have captioned videotapes, nor do they have other backup plans such as an on-call counselor who can sign and come in as needed to work with deaf patients. All too often, the burden of providing on-going treatment is placed on the interpreter's (or the interpreter coordinator's) shoulders instead of on the management of the treatment program, where it rightfully belongs. The treatment program should have a contingency plan in place; however, programs are usually supported by limited funds and are often unable to provide sufficient alternative options or back-up interpreters for emergencies.

A good interpreter with experience working in substance abuse treatment programs may encourage the client to interact with the hearing patients in the program and will assist with all such interchanges. Less experienced interpreters may simply chat with the client themselves while waiting for the next activity or event. In these chats, the interpreter and client may develop a co-dependent relationship, with the interpreter offering advice when it is the counselors, the other patients, and staff who should be in the support role. This may not be the interpreter's fault, because a deaf client may want to spend as much time as possible with someone who can sign. The client feels lonely because all the other patients are hearing and do not know his language.

Deaf people may only feel safe and comfortable talking directly with a person who is fluent in ASL. Many deaf people are not used to working with interpreters, especially for intimate conversation about sensitive subjects. Deaf people do not generally seek help from people with whom they cannot communicate easily, so it can be important to question deaf clients about their previous experience in working with sign language interpreters. It may be necessary to provide training for them about how to work with sign language interpreters so as to enhance relationships with the counselor and other patients in the program.

Volunteer Interpreters

In the early 1970s in the Washington, DC area, all of the sign language interpreters at AA meetings were volunteers. They sometimes assumed the attitude that they were "helping" those poor deaf people; however, because most of them had the best of intentions, they were accepted by recovering deaf people at the time. Deaf people felt that they could "get by" in the recovery process with help from these volunteer interpreters. They did not understand the principle of communication access.

Many of those early volunteer interpreters were fluent in ASL, although a few used signed English. Some were committed to interpret at many meetings — about five to six meetings a week — all around the metropolitan area. In fact, there was even a volunteer interpreting coordinator helping to work out a schedule. The recovering deaf AA members showed their gratitude for these services by providing annual banquets or parties in their honor. At the same time, the deaf AA members sometimes felt obligated towards these interpreters and had many ambivalent emotions.

On the plus side, it is important to mention that during this early period, recovering deaf people did not have to worry about finding interpreters for meetings, planning fundraisers, or paying for these interpreters themselves. They just focused on staying sober and tried to learn as much as possible from hearing AA members about the 12 Step program.

Paid Interpreters

Today, most interpreters have graduated from Interpreter Training Programs and regard themselves as professionals. Charges for certified and even non-certified interpreters may range from $45 to $80 per hour in Washington, DC. Understandably, many small recovering groups and self-help groups cannot pay this amount, nor can the group justify the cost for just one deaf AA member. Sometimes AA members who have learned some signs offer to provide limited interpreting services. Unfortunately, two of the common problems with these well-meaning volunteer interpreters are speed and accuracy. A deaf person in recovery may receive inadequate information because so much is lost, and the hearing AA members do not get enough information to know or understand the deaf member. There are some skilled and certified interpreters who do volunteer, but most of the time, they limit their interpreting to a few weeks or months on a regular basis. Very few are able or willing to commit to on-going interpreting at regular meetings.

Some student interpreters volunteer in order to gain experience and to learn more about deaf people. Most of them have beginning interpreter skills and are not certified. Special care must be taken when scheduling volunteers because some are not ready to deal with the emotional issues that come up in AA meetings. However, with appropriate referrals from experienced interpreting coordinators or from an interpreter training program, there are some skilled volunteers who are willing and able to provide services at these meetings.

Funding for Interpreting Services

Today, interpreters usually expect to be paid to work at AA meetings. There are several sources for interpreting funds. One is state government funding. California and Texas have paid for interpreters at AA meetings for the past ten or more years. Other states sometimes pay for periods of one or two years. Funds have been cut from state budgets for various economic reasons. Sometimes the funds are limited and provide interpreting services for only one or two AA meetings a week.

Funds may also be provided by county governments and distributed through local Alcohol and Drug Abuse Councils. Usually these funds are restricted to meetings in that particular county. Some recovering deaf people who live in the neighboring counties travel long distances to these meetings because there are no interpreted meetings in their own area.

AA and other self-help groups sometimes set aside funds for sign language interpreters. One of the principles of Alcoholics Anonymous is that each group be self-supporting. If one or more deaf members attend a specific group regularly, requesting an interpreter, the group may elect to pay the interpreter out of their collected funds. The drawback here is that the deaf members must first develop a relationship with the group before such a commitment can be obtained. This means the deaf person must pay for the interpreter at first, or that the interpreter volunteers time until the group can agree to accept this responsibility.

Jason's AA group agreed to pay for an interpreter on a weekly basis. Ron, the interpreter, would come to meetings and wait about 15 minutes or so after the meeting started. Ron would leave if no deaf member showed up, but the group would be charged for his time. After Jason missed a few meetings in a row, the group asked the interpreter to stop coming. Later, when Jason returned, he found no interpreter. Hearing members are able to miss several meetings or more and then come back to the group when they want to. But for Jason, the situation is more complicated. If he returns to the meeting and finds that there is no interpreting, he may just give up and not come back. If he stays on, he will probably have to justify his absence to the other members. He will have to make another request for the group to pay for interpreting and may be required to make a commitment to the group to come regularly.

Should AA Groups Share the Costs of Interpreting Services?

Sometimes hearing AA members object to this expense and insist that the recovering deaf members bring their own interpreters. Most recovering deaf members cannot afford to pay for interpreters, and feel overwhelmed by the problems of recruiting qualified volunteers. If they are fortunate to live in bigger cities or towns where there are interpreting training programs, they may be able to contact these programs for assistance. Even deaf members in these large cities, who have been paying for interpreting services, face difficulties in getting their own home group to share some financial responsibilities. Here is a story that occurred in 1997.

A group of deaf AA members have been attending an "Eastside" group AA meeting in Washington, DC for a long time. The deaf members have been paying for interpreters. After a few years, they thought that this group should share the responsibility for costs, because the interpreters also allowed the hearing members to have access to the deaf members' sharing in addition to providing access to theirs.

One day the deaf members brought it up to the group after the AA meeting and suggested that the group share the cost as much as possible. The group decided to select a committee of three to look into the matter and present a proposal. All of these committee members were hearing. One of the members of the group requested that they include one of the two deaf members. The committee refused.

It took the committee about a month to decide, while the deaf members continued to pay the interpreting costs. At the next business meeting after an AA meeting, the committee announced that they decided not to provide money, nor help with the costs for the deaf members to have a sign language interpreter. In explaining why, they used an analogy, saying that the AA group was not responsible to pay for the costs of a ramp for a wheelchair user to go down to a basement meeting. Such costs were beyond their ability to pay.

The deaf members were surprised that the group decision was based on the recommendation of these three members of the committee. There was no vote from the group. The deaf members found it sad that the group was putting all the responsibility for interpreting costs on them. Yet, some of the hearing members had chosen to use the interpreter to talk with the deaf members before or after the meetings. They had access to communication with the deaf members and yet did not want to pay for this.

How did the deaf members feel? They felt sad and hurt that no one in this group took a stronger stand in opposition to the decision of a three-member committee. They felt invalidated — that their sharing in meetings was unimportant and unnecessary to the hearing members. They were not sure about what they would do. One alternative was to find another AA group that might be more willing to share the responsibility. They contacted the National Association of the Deaf Law Center for advice.

The Law Center explained that the ADA ruling does not apply to many AA meeting groups because they are private groups, not receiving any outside funding. [The ADA does, however, apply to AA groups established at hospitals or other institutions that fall under ADA and Section 504 regulations, see chapter 8 for more information.] So, the deaf members decided to change meeting places and stopped attending the Eastside meetings.

These deaf members attended various other group meetings, but still paid for the interpreting services themselves. As time went by, an increasing number of new deaf members began attending the same meetings. Although some of the deaf members were still ambivalent on this issue, they continued to share full responsibility for these services.

Betty G. Miller

They thought that after they attended new meetings on a regular basis, they can again make a request for the group to share the expenses.

Some interpreters would accept lower rates or even not accept payment at all once they learned that the deaf members were paying for themselves. Some interpreting agencies may work out special rates for these services and/or find fluent interpreters who are willing to work on a pro bono basis. The resolution of this issue depends on understanding and willingness among deaf and hearing members of AA groups, sign language interpreters, and sign language agencies.

Need for Boundaries

Lack of clarity about boundaries can lead to a co-dependent relationship between an interpreter and a recovering deaf person. The interpreter's professional and social life can become tangled in confusing ways. For example, at an alcohol and drug treatment program, Jason, a recovering deaf patient, talks with Gina, an interpreter, while waiting for his counseling session. Jason starts to share some personal experiences. Gina feels uncomfortable but finds herself in a dilemma. In the deaf community, it is common to share personal experiences with interpreter friends because they can communicate fluently in ASL. Such conversations also include updates about events or news in the community. Gina knows this and does not want to offend Jason by telling him to wait to share his feelings with his counselor. Instead, she listens, and tries not to get involved. When they go into the counseling session, Jason does not mention to the counselor some significant information that he shared with Gina. Gina's mixed and uncomfortable feelings affect her interpreting work whenever she is in a session with the hearing counselor and Jason. She is not sure of her allegiances or her responsibilities.

Furthermore, Gina may internalize Jason's feelings of pain. She is committed to abide by the interpreter's Code of Ethics, so she cannot share her feelings with anyone outside of the meeting. Gina, however, needs support to deal with her own unresolved issues. This conflict may lead to a "burnout" situation for her, and she may quit working with Jason after a few sessions.

Interpreter as Barrier

In treatment programs, friendly relationships among in-patients are encouraged. Sometimes a deaf client will try to substitute a personal relationship with the interpreter. Jason does this to avoid the issues that arise trying to pursue the friendships that he needs to maintain his sobriety. He may feel he is unable to develop any relationship with his fellow hearing patients because of cultural differences or his past experiences with hearing people. He does not share these feelings with his counselor.

We have already mentioned that the interpreter is almost always a part of the deaf community. A deaf client may share information in private conversation, yet still feel concern about privacy issues because he knows the interpreter personally and attends parties where the interpreter is often present. This inhibits sharing personal experiences during some meetings. Even though the interpreter is bound to confidentiality, the feelings of discomfort and mistrust take over.

Interpreters have been known to make unwanted and inappropriate advances toward the deaf person or other group members before or after AA meetings. One interpreter approached a deaf woman client, flirted boldly, and asked her to go out with him. This left her with the dilemma of reporting him and losing interpreting services, or continuing in a very uncomfortable situation. On the other hand, some members of AA or NA groups will approach a deaf member with notes asking personal questions about an attractive interpreter or requesting an introduction. It is not difficult to imagine how awkward the deaf person feels in this kind of situation.

Hearing AA/NA members sometimes think they are qualified to judge the interpreter's skills even though they have little or no knowledge or experience with sign language and interpreting. They may even defend interpreters from criticism, as if deaf people do not know how to make such judgements for themselves.

It is also not unusual for hearing AA members who are curious about deaf people to address their questions about ASL, Deaf culture, and deafness to the interpreter. They ignore Jason who is standing right there. This makes Jason feel inferior. The interpreter is in the position of importance and power. Jason feels like his existence is irrelevant. Likewise, some interpreting service agencies do not follow requests for certified and qualified interpreters for AA/NA meetings and send non-certified interpreters. Occasionally, interpreters will show up late, or not at all, without notification or apology.

Deaf clients may contact the service agency to express their concerns and and anger, but more often the agencies and interpreters do not receive complaints directly from consumers. The deaf members who depend on them for communication access are afraid to report to the referral agencies about the interpreter. They feel that they need interpreters and fear that if they express grievances, they will lose the services. They tell themselves that even unskilled interpreters are "better than nothing." The deaf members swallow their complaints and complain to their deaf AA friends only. If a deaf member can no longer tolerate certain interpreters, this person may stop attending the meetings or try to change the days or locations of the meetings.

On the other hand, there are times when a deaf person does not show up for designated, interpreted AA meetings. This may discourage or anger the interpreters and weaken their commitment to attend these meetings, even though the hearing members do not always attend every meeting. Sometimes, these situations may be masking a power struggle in the relationship between the interpreters and recovering deaf persons.

Recovering Interpreters

Sometimes, interpreters who regularly work for an alcohol and drug treatment program or AA meetings will run up against their own addiction and co-dependency problems. They may eventually enter their own recovery program. Should a recovering interpreter work at AA meetings? Sometimes, sponsors or AA members encourage recovering interpreters to fulfill their AA services responsibility by doing some interpreting at AA meetings. However, these interpreters may have issues, including resentment, anger, and relationship problems with deaf people that are unresolved. Their unresolved issues may interfere with their own or the deaf person's recovery process. Because of these unresolved personal issues, it is recommended that a newly recovering AA member who is also an interpreter try to avoid interpreting at AA meetings until they are farther along in recovery. They should also be cautious and try not to attend the same meetings as the deaf members.

Deaf people in recovery always face a dilemma about communication access. It is not only a language issue, but also extends to ongoing conflicts and cultural differences. Deaf people gradually learn to understand and accept that interpreting is a necessary tool for communication access and developing relationships with hearing AA members. They have to be willing to risk and take responsibility to ensure confidentiality. They need to be direct and work with interpreters to resolve whatever interpreting issues arise, making every effort to maintain a professional relationship.

Alcoholism and drug abuse are serious matters of life and death. It used to be that an alcoholic or drug user would go to any length to get a drink or get high. In recovery this same attitude can accomplish positive change: he or she must be willing to go to any length to stay sober. Until there are other high-tech ways to replace interpreters, human beings, with all their contradictions, are the only viable means of achieving accessible communication.

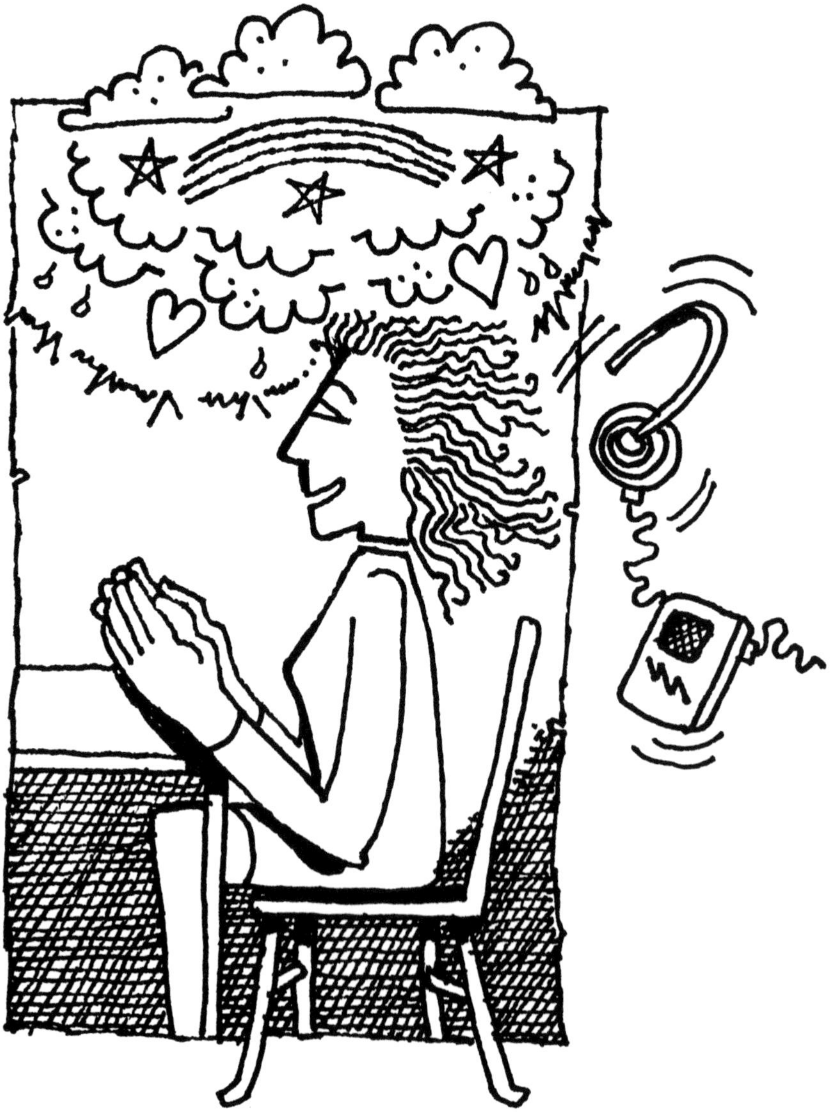

Chapter Eight

Access Laws: Section 504 and ADA

Dr. Betty G. Miller, Advocate

Since 1979, Dr. Betty G. Miller has been a persistent and effective advocate for communication access to substance abuse recovery services, including 12 Step meetings. Although she had little advocacy experience when she first approached a member of the San Francisco County Alcohol Abuse Council, she was able to convince the Council that there was a need for interpreting services at AA meetings in the city. Within a year, the funding for these services was made available, and deaf people could attend regularly scheduled interpreted AA meetings in the Bay area.

Dr. Miller moved to Los Angeles in 1981 and again found it necessary to advocate for appropriate services. In 1983 and 1984, Dr. Miller, with support from Leo Mouton of the Greater Los Angeles Council on Deafness (GLAD), began corresponding with the Council of Alcohol and Drug Abuse Services of Los Angeles County. At the time, the county provided no accessible treatment services for deaf persons with alcohol and drug problems. When these efforts brought no results, Dr. Miller filed a complaint with the Office of Civil Rights (OCR) in California claiming a violation of Section 504. After prolonged discussion and a review of Dr. Miller's documents, the staff of the OCR decided a violation had occurred and confronted the County Council. Negotiations continued until 1985. Finally, the Council conceded and agreed to begin providing funds for interpreters so that deaf and hard of hearing people could have equal access to all treatment programs in the county. Today, because of this action, there are accessible treatment programs and 12 Step self-help groups for deaf and hard of hearing people in the Los Angeles area. Where once there were none, there are now at least two treatment programs completely accessible to all deaf persons in California, plus as many as 25 interpreted self-help meetings a week.

In 1992, Dr. Miller once again filed a complaint, this time for a violation under Title III of the Americans with Disabilities Act (ADA). In her complaint, she charged an educational non-profit organization in Washington, DC with refusing to provide interpreters for educational classes required for re-certification of addiction counselors. After two years and repeated attempts to resolve this issue through letters to the organization, the non-profit still refused to comply, claiming undue hardship and financial burden. Dr. Miller contacted the Department of Justice with her concerns, and sent copies of the letters documenting her claim. The Department of Justice reviewed the situation and concluded that violations of Title III of the ADA and Section 504 of the Rehabilitation Act of 1973 had, indeed, occurred. Six months later, the organization finally agreed to provide interpreters at their seminars and programs for Dr. Miller and other interested deaf participants.

Advocacy

The message from these stories is that any motivated consumer can and should file a complaint with the Civil Rights Division of the U.S. Department of Justice if there is evidence of a violation of Section 504 of the Rehabilitation Act of 1973, the Americans with Disabilities Act of 1990 (ADA) or both. Consumers must have documented evidence to show the Department of Justice that a violation has occurred. Even if the action is successful, it may take months or years for an investigation to be conducted and real changes implemented. Although advocacy requires a lot of time and perseverance, the results are well worth it. To be a successful advocate, it is necessary to know your rights and to become familiar with the laws that protect them.

Section 504

Section 504 of the Rehabilitation Act of 1973 requires that federal programs that receive federal funding be accessible to handicapped persons. The U.S. Department of Human Services (HHS) regulations to Section 504 require provision of necessary auxiliary aids, such as sign language interpreters, to ensure equal access to these programs. These regulations specify that a recipient of federal funding that employs fifteen or more persons shall provide appropriate auxiliary aids to persons with impaired sensory, manual, or speaking skills, so as to give such persons an equal opportunity to benefit from the service in question.

Section 504 also covers communication between deaf persons and health care providers, and the Department of Health and Human Services Office of Civil Rights has determined that effective communication must be provided at "critical points" during hospitalization, including substance abuse inpatient treatment programs. "Critical points" are defined as those times when important medical information is communicated, such as at admission, when explaining medical procedures, when informed consent is required for treatment, and at discharge. Furthermore, under Section 504, ASL has been defined as…

> …a manually communicated language distinct from English and whose idioms and concepts are not directly translatable into English. It uses different structure, grammar, and syntax than English, and is as much a foreign language to English speaking persons as is French or German. Conversely, English is equally foreign to most deaf persons who rely on ASL for communication. It is a common misconception that "sign language" is merely a pantomime of the English language and is therefore easily understandable in print if not through sound. ASL sentences do not follow English sequential patterns. As a

result, direct translation of English, as with written notes, into ASL will not necessarily convey the intended message. Similarly, much of English idiomatic speech would be lost on the ASL user, whose frame of reference for idioms is significantly different from hearing persons.

(U.S. Department of Health and Human Services, Office of Civil Rights, Region III, 1991).

A qualified sign language interpreter is one who, "...is able to interpret effectively, accurately and impartially both receptively and expressively, using any necessary specialized vocabulary." (Section 504, Effective Communications and Health Care providers.)

The Americans with Disabilities Act of 1990

In addition to Section 504 obligations, hospitals, including inpatient, outpatient, and emergency treatment settings, have an additional federal obligation to provide auxiliary aids and services to disabled patients under the Americans with Disabilities Act (ADA). Title III of the ADA covers every public accommodation, including health care providers, regardless of whether that entity receives federal financial assistance, and regardless of the number of employees in the facility. Title II of the ADA covers every public healthcare facility operated by a state or local government entity.

In his presentation, "Empowerment through Advocacy by Deaf People for Meaningfully Accessible Substance Abuse/Alcoholism Treatment" at the Substance Abuse and Recovery Conference, June, 1990, Dr. William P. McCrone declared,

> ...the Americans with Disabilities Act is the most important federal legislation for people with disabilities since the 1973 Rehabilitation Act. Both laws have applicability in the challenge of getting more and better services for deaf alcoholics and deaf addicts.

The purpose of the Americans with Disabilities Act of 1990 is to grant civil rights protections to individuals with disabilities. The ADA guarantees equal opportunity for individuals with disabilities in employment, public accommodations, transportation, state and local government services, and telecommunications. There are several categories of protections designed to accommodate various special needs of persons with disabilities, separated into "titles."

Title III of the ADA prohibits discrimination on the basis of disability by private entities in places of public accommodation. Title III requires that all new places of public accommodation and commercial facilities be designed and constructed so as to be readily accessible and usable by persons with disabilities, It also requires that examinations or courses related to licensing or certification for professional and trade purposes be accessible.

Title III applies to all health care providers, regardless of the size of the office or the number of employees. It applies to providers of nursing homes and to providers of physical and mental health care. Hospitals, substance abuse treatment programs, psychiatric and psychological services, offices of private physicians, dentists, and health clinics are included among the health care providers covered by the ADA.

For example, a health care provider in a substance abuse treatment program must be able to communicate effectively with clients, family members, and other deaf individuals who are seeking or receiving its services. Such individuals may not always be "patients" of the health care provider. Family involvement is an important part of any successful treatment program. If an educational class about substance abuse is offered to family members as a service at a drug treatment program, deaf parents, spouses, siblings, or children must be given the same opportunity to benefit from this class as hearing family members. Auxiliary aids or services will be needed to make this possible. Appropriate auxiliary aids and services may include qualified interpreters, assistive listening devices, notetakers, written materials, television decoders, and telecommunications devices for the deaf (TTYs).

The health care provider cannot charge a patient for the costs of providing auxiliary aids and services, either directly or through the patient's insurance carrier. However, the ADA does not require the provision of any auxiliary aid or service that would result in "an undue burden or in a fundamental alteration in the nature of the services provided" by the health care provider. AA/NA and similar self-help groups are not generally covered by Title III unless they are operated by a hospital or similar organization, or institution. In situations where Section 504 or the ADA does apply, organizing to file a complaint is the next step.

Approaching independent groups which are not subject to the ADA or Section 504 requires persuasive advocacy rather than legal arguments, as explained by Sarah Geer, attorney at law, of the National Association of the Deaf Law Center in her letter to a deaf AA member from the Washington, DC area (used with permission):

> I would recommend talking to them about the fundamental principles of AA as a *mutual* self-help group, intended to help *each other* achieve/maintain sobriety, etc. The interaction and the mutual support are essential to AA success — if not, then each member would just be sitting at home alone thinking about sobriety, instead of participating in and benefitting from the group itself. The extra dollar or so that you are asking for members to chip in is a very small but critical way for them to include the deaf AA members. [I also recommend] the approach of explaining that *they* benefit from your participation, just as you benefit from their participation. People forget that the interpreter is a two-way street, not just giving you the ability to communicate with them but giving them the ability to communicate with you as well.

Organizing

Dr. William McCrone, professor of counseling at Gallaudet University, has identified four components essential to successful advocacy efforts. They are structure, process, relationships, and accountability.

In doing advocacy work, it is important not to tackle the job alone. The structure is a means to inform, recruit, and organize others to join the effort. The process involves setting up a mechanism for collecting information, clarifying a purpose, and for developing and evaluating an action plan.

An advocate has to build relationships with friends and opponents. This means getting to know politicians, bureaucrats, and staff people as well as becoming familiar with local media, including newspapers and television news programs. Networking with individuals and organizations such as the National Association of the Deaf can help to achieve advocacy goals. Finally every step must be evaluated to learn from mistakes and build on successes.

Advocacy and Empowerment

Personal empowerment is a challenge for many recovering deaf people who have little or no feelings of self esteem. First of all, many deaf people do not have opportunities to hone their decision-making skills or learn from their mistakes as children. Often their parents, medical professionals, or educators make decisions with the best of intentions but with no knowledge of deaf issues or Deaf culture.

Dr. William McCrone, in his discussion regarding the lack advocacy in the deaf community (McCrone, 1990, p. 107) asks, "Where do deaf children develop the basic skills to become political activists? Where do deaf children learn to make decisions? Where do they learn to develop a consensus among deaf peers whom they cherish? Where do they develop the confidence to trust their own judgments? Where do the deaf kids meet adult deaf role models? Where do the deaf kids get experience in 'leadership training'?"

For some deaf people, anger is their only tool. They are often impulsive, making demands and experiencing many frustrations. When nothing immediately results from their actions, they give up. They need to do away with their "learned helplessness" (McCrone, 1979), and accept the responsibility that they can make a difference.

They need to be involved in the deaf community where they can find role models and develop new skills. It is possible, but it is not easy.

To be fully empowered, deaf people need to be educated about themselves as proud deaf people by learning about ASL and Deaf culture. Even in a recovery program deaf people encounter many barriers because they belong to a small and misunderstood minority. They need to develop basic skills in order to become effective as their own advocates. For example, they can learn that their anger can be used in constructive ways. If a program provides leadership training, deaf clients can learn to set priorities and make action plans. As they gain experience, they will learn to trust their own judgments and make decisions.

Deaf people, even in the early stages of recovery, are often urged to become involved in advocacy and recruitment of other deaf people into alcohol and drug treatment programs. Deaf people do need to learn to advocate for themselves to obtain all the services they need for their recovery, but some people are not ready for these activities. They need to build up self-esteem and confidence first. It may require five or more years in the recovery process to develop such skills and become empowered. In time, they will need to take up responsibilities in advocating for themselves to achieve what they want and to break through attitude and communication barriers.

Carl

After a few months of sobriety, Carl felt much stronger and became involved in advocating for sign language interpreters at AA meetings in his area. Although he was sober, Carl was an angry man with many unresolved issues about his deafness. If he did not succeed in getting what he wanted, he walked out of the AA business meetings and complained bitterly to any AA member who would listen. In the meantime, he did not have the time to work on the 12 Steps, his own issues, and his own recovery. At first, he blamed the AA business members for not being cooperative and not listening to him. He became so angry that he stopped attending AA meetings. He had forgotten that the most important principle of recovery was maintaining his own sobriety and taking care of himself. Carl became overwhelmed with frustrations at not achieving his goals for accessibility and eventually relapsed.

Recovery is a process that does not happen overnight. Often a substance abuser requires many years to develop a healthy attitude towards day to day activities and the skills for coping in all areas of life. The most difficult aspect of recovery, which requires substantial courage, is the process of making changes to the inner life of the recovering person. For a recovering deaf person like Carl, time, patience, and a lot of personal work are required before he can deal with the stress involved in advocacy without endangering his sobriety and confidence. He will need education, support, and validation from his AA sponsors, friends, and other deaf leaders, as well as support from the law centers which work closely with deaf people on access issues and discrimination.

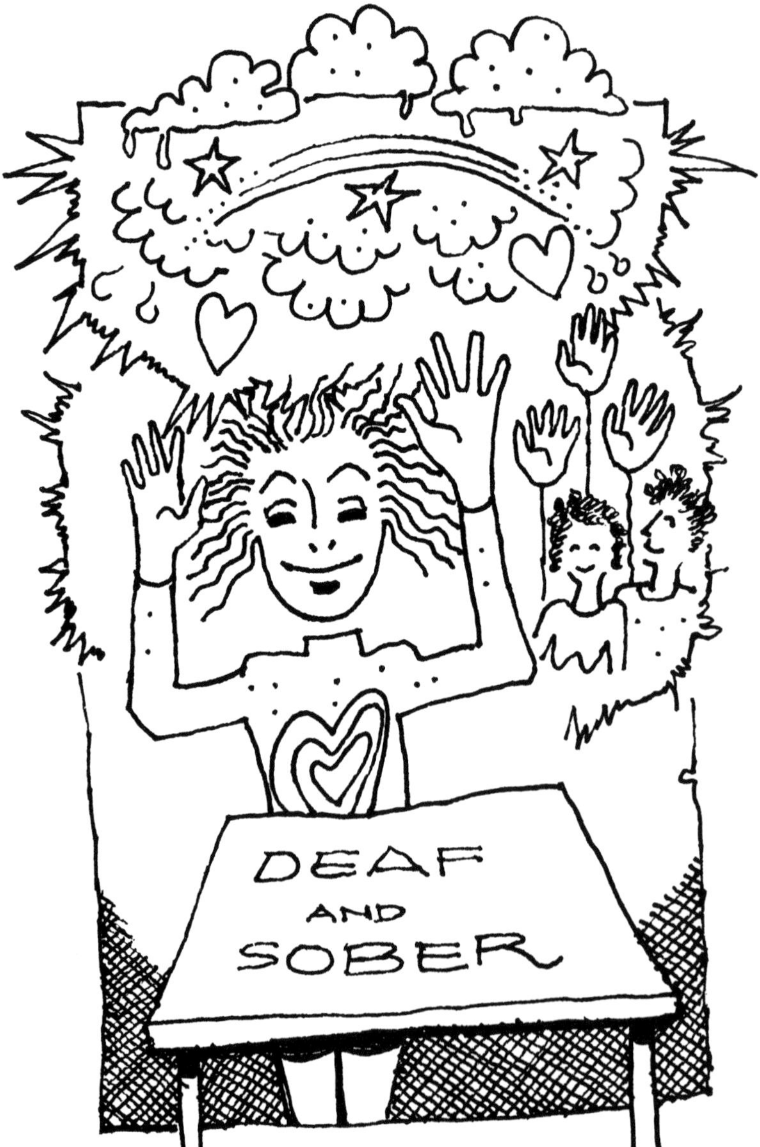
DEAF
AND
SOBER

Chapter Nine

Friends, Family, and Spirituality

Terence Gorski, author of *Passages through Recovery: An Action Plan for Preventing Relapses* explains that,

> We (as recovering addicts) need to remember that chemical addiction including alcoholism causes brain dysfunction, and brain dysfunction disorganizes the personality. Many of us believe that as soon as we are sober, we should be instantly psychologically healthy. The long term brain function (post-acute withdrawal) can prevent us from being fully functional for periods of six to eighteen months into recovery. As the symptoms of brain dysfunction begin to clear up, our pre-addictive personality traits return. We return to the same level of psychological health we had before we became addicted. This is why the Twelve Step program places so much emphasis on identifying and correcting our character defects. Character defects can be described as ongoing psychological problems. Some of these problems were caused by our addiction itself. Some were present before we ever became addicted.

People in the deaf community usually know when other deaf people have serious alcohol and drug problems. But they need to recognize that a recovering deaf person is not the same person as the one they knew who was using and drinking. Deaf addicts who are in recovery need to be able to turn to members of the deaf community for positive support. Their families and friends need to be loving, open, and willing to make an effort to understand. Recovering addicts should be acknowledged with respect.

Friends and family members sometimes have a hard time understanding that recovering addicts who are attending AA meetings and working on the 12 Steps have committed themselves to an on-going process. As explained above, the addict's brain functioning takes a long time to become clear and become fully recovered. It takes more time to admit to personal weaknesses and to change lifelong habits such as negative thinking and having self-defeating and self-destructive behaviors. It may help friends and spouses to be supportive if they remind themselves that the recovery process really includes the whole family. One of the reasons that recovering addicts commit themselves to treatment, which may include AA meetings on a daily basis for the first two or three years, is to learn to function better in family and intimate relationships. Sometimes the process may take longer for recovering deaf people, because they are not able to attend as many meetings and work on the Steps as often as hearing people can.

Family members and friends can get help through AA, ACOA, and from Al-Anon groups which are there to help them focus on their own needs. Counseling for both individuals and for couples is encouraged, in order for each partner to function better in the relationship. In this way, the process of healing and recovery touches everyone involved.

Letting Friends Know

"People who have achieved a healthy and well-balanced family and intimate life are able to communicate openly and honestly with the people they love. They are able to let others know who they are, including both their strengths and weaknesses." (Gorski, 1989.)

In many cases, the changes from alcoholic family behavior to a well-balanced family life are possible with appropriate family counseling, but the process of recovering will take a long time for the whole family. Friends from the deaf community can lend support and understanding. However, the desire to keep alcoholism a secret is strong within the deaf community. This attitude needs to change so that support can be provided. We need to let friends know.

For example, deaf people give support to friends who have a serious disease, helping until the friend recovers. Why can't deaf people offer the same support to their recovering friends? Wouldn't a recovering deaf person reach out to their deaf friends and ask for help from time to time, along with developing new hearing friends from Alcoholics Anonymous? Perhaps the deaf friends don't know what to do? How about arranging a training session for these friends, teaching them how to provide support and become "buddies"? Education on recovery, substance abuse, and alcoholism can be provided.

Anonymous

What is "anonymous"? The dictionary explains that the word means "having an unknown or unacknowledged name." In Alcoholics Anonymous, this is redefined to mean that it does not matter who you are, what you do for a living, your race, religion, nationality, or your social status. The sole purpose of membership is get and give help and support, and the only requirement is a desire to stop drinking. It is no secret that each member is trying to recover from the disease of alcoholism or chemical dependency. For every recovering deaf addict, each day of accomplished sobriety is a miracle.

Deaf people may want to provide support to recovering people in the community, but they may not know what to do. Before they can provide support, they need to recognize that the process of recovering includes learning to think clearly, to manage feelings and emotions, and to manage stress. Friends need to be patient and understanding, and are encouraged attend Al-Anon meetings themselves.

Twelve Step programs offer three primary tools to help the alcoholic through recovery. They are AA/NA meeting attendance, sponsorship, and slogans. It is encouraged that they attend as many meetings (including interpreted) as possible. A sponsor (deaf or hearing) can provide one-to-one contact with the newly recovering deaf person who may need help during the rough times. Slogans, such as "One Day at a Time," "Turn It Over," "Easy Does It," and "Live and Let Live," become reminders, code words to check your behavior and work the Steps.

Friends may find that a deaf AA/NA member's behavior is immature and awkward during the early stages of recovery, regardless of their age. Recovering people learn to assume responsiblity for all of their actions, both good and bad. Do not expect them to become "magically" recovered in a short time. They cannot. To maintain sobriety is essential. They cannot have even one drink. Abstinence is essential. They also need to change their lifestyles. With all this in mind, friends can provide support by being there, and giving love and care.

Service Providers

There are service providers who also are part of the deaf community. They work directly with various kinds of deaf people, including mental health services serving deaf people, the deaf units of the Rehabilitation Services Administration, other deaf service providers (such as counselors, advocates, independent living counselors, and social workers), and universities and residential schools for the deaf. They are essential to the recovery process for many deaf persons in that they assist with personal counseling, career placement, skills training, education, and other related services that may enhance the self-esteem and self sufficiency of recovering people. Unfortunately, many of these service providers are not knowledgeable enough about substance abuse and its impact on their clients in recovery. Some may become impatient, puzzled, and frustrated with their clients. They sometimes think that now that their clients are sober, they should become responsible, mature, and capable in a short period of time, right after leaving the drug treatment program.

It is essential that recovering clients receive understanding and support. A temporary job, for example, could be arranged immediately for clients. This will help them to develop skills such as working with co-workers and supervisors.

Fortunately, training programs for service providers today are including substance abuse as an essential part of professional knowledge. Service providers are also encouraged to be more involved during their client's last few weeks in the treatment programs, when aftercare plans are being arranged.

Professional Deaf People in Recovery

There may be recovering, professional deaf people who attend interpreted AA meetings, but who do not want other recovering deaf members to know. Usually their profession is in the helping field, where they may have recovering clients who also attend AA meetings. In principle, no one can be excluded from the meetings. The question, however, is how can recovering deaf members share their problems, which may include work situations, if one or two recovering deaf clients attend the same meetings? Do these professional deaf members have a right to reserve certain meetings for themselves? Because it is an interpreted meeting, and there are very few interpreted meetings weekly, do the recovering deaf members still have the right not to share information about this particular meeting with other recovering deaf members? It is a dilemma, and sometimes the other recovering deaf members may not understand or care about the situation that the professional deaf members face.

Why is it so important to many deaf people to keep their problems with alcohol or drugs a secret? Why are many deaf people so fearful of "gossip" circulating in the community about their recovery? Perhaps it is really shame about past experiences that cause addicts, their family members and friends to want to keep their lives hidden. Addiction, including alcoholism and substance abuse, is a disease that cannot be cured, but it can be controlled. From the beginning of recovery, the focus must be on staying sober and on learning to accept ourselves and not be ashamed of our disease.

Keeping a secret separates deaf addicts from other members of the deaf community. Remaining anonymous keeps a recovering person separate not only from others, but also inside themselves. They cannot disclose who they truly are. This means not acknowledging an important part of the person's true identity. To keep such as a secret requires them to deny that the problem exists, even after they have become sober. One deaf AA member stated that he could not separate alcoholism from himself as it is an important part of who he is in becoming a whole person.

The deaf community usually knows who these people are. It needs to recognize that a recovering deaf person is not the same person who was using and drinking. The recovery process and change may take a very long time, though deaf addicts who are in recovery need to be able to turn to members of the deaf community for positive support. Their families and friends need to be loving, open and willing to make an effort to understand. If the recovering addicts are willing to be identified, their names should be acknowledged with respect..

Many deaf addicts are grateful and proud of their sobriety. They are courageous people who have faced many challenges, broken through many barriers, and made serious changes in order to live a drug-free life. They deserve to be respected and applauded as much as other deaf leaders in the deaf community. Because of AA principles, they cannot, and should not, be awarded with trophies or similar awards, but they still can be acknowledged through constant support throughout the deaf community.

Spirituality

Amanda's Story

I have been in recovery for over six years. I started drinking when I was nine years old. Before long, booze had become my "best friend." I loved and trusted booze more than anything else to take away my emotional pain and make me feel good. Little did I know that in later years, booze and drugs would betray me and become my worst enemy. By the age of 20, I did not know who I was anymore. I did not care if I lived or died. By this time, I had lost everything I owned and was on my way to prison. I had no hope that I could change as I had tried so many times to quit and better my life, but time and time again I failed. I was physically sick, emotionally dead, and spiritually lost.

Ten years ago, I had my first experience with recovery, but it did not last. After going through treatment the first time, I relapsed and went back to drinking and drugging. I did not understand much about the process of recovery due to the lack of communication. I did not have sign language interpreters in this treatment program. I left there still feeling that I was on the outside looking in, isolated even when I was among a group of people in a room. I managed to stay dry for six months after treatment, but I was unable to learn to change myself or improve myself physically, emotionally, mentally, and spiritually.

After six months of being dry, I made the choice to drink and drug again because it was something I knew how to do well. I knew that booze and drugs could take away the pain, loneliness, and frustration that I was feeling. I had not learned any other way to cope with my life. To really recover, one must have access to communication and be able to share thoughts and feelings, but at that time I did not know how to advocate for myself to get communication access at AA meetings. I did not have any recovering deaf role model in my home area to assist me with a 12 Step program. After a long relapse, I almost died. With the grace of God, I made a decision to go to another treatment program and this time, the program provided sign language interpreters.

After this treatment, I lived in a halfway house for women for three months. Interpreters were also provided there. With good communication, I was able to see the light and value of sobriety. I finally understood what I had to do with my life. Accessible communication helped me build relationships with new people who are in recovery. I also met new deaf friends who are in recovery. Also, I learned how to advocate for my rights so that I could continue with my process of recovery, including 12 Step meetings, workshops, therapy, sponsors, shared experiences, and even learning about spirituality.

Now after six clean and sober years, I have so much in my life for which to be grateful. I now have a close and wonderful relationship with my family. I have friends who understand and support me, offering me unconditional love. I learned to trust them, and above all, my higher power. The road I travelled in my recovery has not been an easy one. There have been many ups and downs, struggles, mistakes, tests of faith and temptations to give up and go back to my old ways, but through their experience, strength, and hope, my deaf and hearing AA friends have shown me how to survive, one day at a time.

If anyone had told me six years ago that all these good things would happen to me, I surely would have laughed in their face out of disbelief. Today, I am truly grateful for my sobriety and Higher Power. Gratitude is not only a feeling, but also an act of faith. It means that I will be giving back to the program of recovery what I have been given.

Higher Power

The words, "higher power" or "God as we understand Him" are mentioned in almost every 12 Step program. It is often difficult for recovering people to understand or to accept the concept that "God is with me at all times." Deaf people, especially, have often had unhappy experiences with misinformed ministers or priests who behave in a condescending manner to deaf members in their congregation. To them, it appears that religion separates God and humans, spirit and body, good and evil, or themselves and other people. For many deaf people, "Higher Power" or "God" is something that is beyond the reach of poor, ignorant, deaf sinners on Earth.

Dr. Jane Hurst, formerly of the Department of Philosophy and Religion, Gallaudet University, spoke about spirituality at a conference, "Substance Abuse and Recovery: Empowerment of Deaf Persons" at Gallaudet University, 1990. She suggested three spiritual practices that can assist the process of recovery:

1) Hearing the Silence — learning how to find inner quiet within yourself that is beyond the "noise" of your mind and emotions

2) Observing yourself — looking at feelings we have about our bodies and our lives. The self-hater needs to be confronted and replaced by a self-observing angel who believes in your ability and guides you throughout the process.

3) Opening your heart — most of our hearts are numb and confused. There is unexpressed pain and grief in our hearts that needs to be released, but the heart is also the meeting place of body, emotion, mind, and spirit. It is the home of the self-observer and the doorway to the Higher Power.

Once Amanda (and other recovering deaf people) accept the basic concept that spirituality is essential for developing peace within, there are several methods to help her in achieving this goal. Prayers and meditation can be useful to express and listen to the inner self. She can also begin each morning by reading day-by-day meditation books such as AA's *24 Hours* book. Amanda may not attend church every week or follow any formal religion, unless she feels she would be nurtured and inspired to continue with her new life. Nevertheless, she learns that a spiritual awakening means a clear understanding of the Steps.

Amanda knows that she needs to continue to work on all of the 12 Steps, one step at a time and one day at a time. She may not accomplish all of her goals or finish these Steps for many of her sober years to come. Her commitment is to improve her ability to cope with life's problems, and to achieve peace within herself day-by-day. The Big Book of *Alcoholics Anonymous* explains that recovering alcoholics strive for "spiritual progress," not spiritual perfection. That is what spirituality means. It is really simple, but often difficult to accomplish. For Amanda and all other deaf and hearing people, it happens only with daily practice of having conscious contact with the inner spirit throughout the recovery process.

Appendix A: The Twelve Steps

Step 1. We admitted we were powerless over alcohol (drugs) — that our lives had become unmanageable.

Step 2. Came to believe that a Power greater than ourselves could restore us to sanity.

Step 3. Made a decision to turn our will and our lives over to care of God as we understood him.

Step 4. Made a searching and fearless moral inventory of ourselves.

Step 5. Admitted to God, to ourselves, and to another human being the exact nature of our wrongs.

Step 6. Were entirely ready to have God remove all these defects of character.

Step 7. Humbly asked Him to remove our shortcomings.

Step 8. Made a list of all persons we had harmed, and became willing to make amends to them all.

Step 9. Made direct amends to such people wherever possible, except when to do so would injure them or others.

Step 10. Continued to take personal inventory and when we were wrong promptly admitted it.

Step 11. Sought through prayer and meditation to improve our conscious contact with God as we understood Him, praying only for knowledge of His will for us and the power to carry that out.

Step 12. Having had a spiritual awakening as the result of these steps, we tried to carry this message to alcoholics and to practice these principles in all our affairs.

(Twelve Traditions and Twelve Steps, AA World Services, Inc., 1973)

Appendix B: The Twelve Traditions

Tradition 1. Our common welfare should come first; personal recovery depends on AA unity.

Tradition 2. For our group purpose there is but one ultimate authority — a loving God as He may express Himself in our group conscience. Our leaders are but trusted servants; they do not govern.

Tradition 3. The only requirement for AA membership is a desire to stop drinking.

Tradition 4. Each group should be autonomous except in matters affecting other groups of AA as a whole.

Tradition 5. Each group has but one primary purpose — to carry its message to the alcoholics who still suffer.

Tradition 6. An AA group ought never endorse, finance, or lend the AA name to any related facility or outside enterprise, lest problems of money, property, and prestige divert us from our primary purpose.

Tradition 7. Every AA group ought to be fully self-supporting, declining outside contributions.

Tradition 8. Alcoholics Anonymous should remain forever nonprofessional but our service centers may employ special workers.

Tradition 9. AA, as such, should never be organized; but we may create service boards or committees directly responsible to those they serve.

Tradition 10. Alcoholics Anonymous has no opinion on outside issues; hence the AA name ought never be drawn into public controversy.

Tradition 11. Our public relations policy is based on attraction rather than promotion; we need always maintain personal anonymity at the level of press, radio, and films.

Tradition 12. Anonymity is the spiritual foundation of all our traditions, ever reminding us to place principles before personalities.

(Twelve Traditions and Twelve Steps, AA World Services, Inc., 1973)

Appendix C: Thirteen Statements of Acceptance for Deaf Persons

Statement 1.	We have no control or power over our alcohol or drug problem.
Statement 2.	Negative emotions destroy only ourselves.
Statement 3.	We will develop a new habit: being happy and peaceful.
Statement 4.	Problems bother us, why? Because we permit them to.
Statement 5.	We are what we think.
Statement 6.	Life can be ordinary, or it can be great.
Statement 7.	Love can change my path in the world.
Statement 8.	The basic object of life is emotional and spiritual growth.
Statement 9.	The past is gone forever.
Statement 10.	We give love, and we will receive twice as much.
Statement 11.	Enthusiasm and willingness are our daily exercises.
Statement 12.	We are good and smart deaf people and have much to give.
Statement 13.	We are responsible for ourselves and our actions.

submitted by Betty G. Miller, Ed.D., C.A.D.C.

Betty G. Miller

These statements were revised and rewritten from the 13 Statements of Acceptance by Women for Sobriety, see below:

1) I have a drinking (life-threatening) problem that once had me.

2) Negative emotions destroy only myself.

3) Happiness is a habit I will develop myself.

4) Problems bother me only to the degree I permit them.

5) I am what I am.

6) Life can be ordinary or it can be great.

7) Love can change the course of my world.

8) The fundamental object of life is emotional and spiritual growth.

9) The past is gone forever.

10) All love given returns two-fold.

11) Enthusiasm is my daily exercise.

12) I am a competent woman and have much to give life.

13) I am responsible for myself and for my actions.

Glossary of Key Terms

ACOA or ACA (Adult Children of Alcoholics): The alcoholic/substance abuse family system is typically centered around the family member who is an alcoholic or drug addict. The children in this family system grow up looking at the world around them for some indication of how to behave, how to feel and how to respond, rather than using their own internal processes.

Aftercare: Aftercare is an umbrella term for any ongoing program for substance abusers after discharge from an alcohol/drug treatment program. The goal of aftercare is maintenance of sobriety.

Al-Anon: Al-Anon members are family members, significant others, and close friends who live with a recovering alcoholic/addict.

Alcohol and Drug Abuse: A disease that causes a person to lose control over the use of alcohol or other drugs. This loss of control causes physical, psychological, social and spiritual problems (Gorski, 1989).

Alcoholics Anonymous: A fellowship composed of members with a desire to stop drinking or using. Its goal is to help other alcoholics to achieve sobriety.

ADA (The Americans with Disabilities Act): Grants civil rights protections to individuals with disabilities. The ADA guarantees equal opportunity for individuals with disabilities in employment, public accommodations, transportation, state and local government services, and telecommunications.

Anonymous in AA: The dictionary explains that the word means "having an unknown or unacknowledged name." Alcoholics Anonymous redefines this to mean that it does not matter who you are, what you do for a living, your race, religion, nationality, or your social status.

Co-dependency: An individual focuses on another person's feelings and behavior more than upon his or her own. One person allows the other's actions, reactions, successes and failures to dominate her life, her energy, and her attention. She neglects her own wants, needs and feelings to spend her time defining, second guessing or attempting to control another person.

Culture: A set of shared values, norms, traditions, customs, arts, history, folklore, and language of a group of people (Orlandi, editor, 1992).

d/Deaf: The lower case "deaf" refers to the audiological condition of not hearing, while the uppercase "Deaf" refers to a particular group of deaf people who share a language — American Sign Language — and culture (Markowitz and Woodward, 1978).

Deaf Culture: Deaf culture consists of American Sign Language (ASL), a set of learned behaviors, and perceptions that shape the values and norms of Deaf people based on their shared or common experiences (Kannapell, 1993).

Detoxification: The main function of the detoxification center is to provide for the physical recovery of alcoholics and drug addicts, sometimes administering medications such as lithium or valium, and helping them to gradually eliminate drugs from their body.

Drug and Alcohol Treatment Programs: These programs provide treatments to alcoholics and addicts to recover from the disease of alcoholism and addiction, for a period of at least one week or more, depending on the severity of the disease and ability to pay.

Drugs: In this book, drugs include narcotics, hallucinogens, alcohol, and amphetamines, both illegal and legal, which are considered mind altering drugs.

Dual Relationship: Counselors blend their professional relationship with a client with another kind of relationship. Dual relationships, which can take many forms, have been called a violation of ethical, legal, and clinical standards (Pope, 1984).

Recovering Alcoholic or Addict: An alcoholic or addict going through a process of recovery. As of now, there is no cure for alcoholism or addiction. There are no "recovered" alcoholics or addicts.

Recovery: A developmental process where addicts pass through a series of stages from simple abstinence to a meaningful and comfortable sobriety.

Relay Service, or Telephone Relay Service (TRS): With the relay service, the deaf person types a message on the TTY to an operator, who reads it aloud to the hearing person without a TTY on the other end. The operator then relays the hearing person's response via TTY. By utilizing the relay system, recovering deaf people and hearing AA members are able to communicate through the telephone.

Sign Language Interpreter: The role of a sign language interpreter in any setting is to transmit messages between the user of sign language and the user of a spoken language.

Sobriety: Living without a need for alcohol and other drugs, as well as healing the damage to our bodies, minds, relationships, and spirit (Gorski, 1989).

TTY or TDD: a telephone device that deaf people use with a keyboard, typing back and forth over the phone lines.

Bibliography

Alcoholics anonymous (3rd ed.). (1979). New York: Alcoholics Anonymous World Services, Inc. [note: also known as "The Big Book."]

Americans with disability act, initial accessibility good but important barriers remain. (1993, May). Report to the Chairman, Subcommittee on Select Education and Civil Rights, Committee on Education and Labor, House of Representatives, United States Government Accounting Office, Washington, DC.

ASL position paper approved by NAD. (1994, March). *The NAD Broadcaster.*

Bissell, L., MD, CAC & Royce, J.E., SJ, Ph.D. (1987). *Ethics for addictions professionals.* Center City, MN: Hazelden Foundation.

Co-dependency: an emerging issue. (1984). Pompano Beach, FL: Health Communications.

Cohen, O. P. (1993). Multicultural education and the deaf community: A conversation about survival. Garretson, M. (ed.), *A deaf American monograph; Deafness: 1993–2013.* p. 23. Silver Spring, MD: The National Association of the Deaf.

Corey, G., Corey, M.S., & Callanan, P. (1992). *Issues and ethics in the helping professions.* Pacific Grove, CA: Brooks and Cole Publishing Co.

Creighton, N. (1995, July/August). 814 Thayer Avenue. *The NAD Broadcaster.*

Essleman, M., & Velez, E. (1994, June 20). Silent screams. *People weekly.*

Fields, R., Ph.D. (1992). *Drugs and alcohol in perspective.* Dubuque, IA: Wm. C. Brown Publishers.

Finkelstein, N., Ph.D., MSW; Duncan, S.A., MSW; Derman, L., MPH, MSW; & Smeltz, J., M.Ed., CAC. (1992). *Getting sober, getting well.* Cambridge, MA: The Women's Alcoholism Program of CASPAR.

Frishberg, N. (1990). *Interpreting: An introduction* (revised ed.). Silver Spring, MD: RID Publications, Registry of Interpreters for the Deaf, Inc.

Gendreau-Weitzel, C. (1992, July 5–8). Co-dependency within the deaf community. *The next step: a national conference focusing on issues related to substance abuse in the deaf and hard of hearing population, conference proceedings.* Washington, DC: College for Continuing Education, Gallaudet University.

Glass, L., & Elliot, H.H., (1994). On signing with a hearing accent. Garretson, M. (ed.). *A deaf American monograph; Deafness: life and culture.* Silver Spring, MD: National Association of the Deaf.

Gorski, T.T. (1989). *Passages through recovery: An action plan for preventing relapse.* Center City, MN: Hazelden Educational Materials.

Guthmann, D., MA, Ed.D., & Sandberg, K., BS, CCDRC. (1997, Jan.–Feb.). Deaf culture and substance abuse. *The counselor.*

Hurst, J. (1990, June 5–9). Spirituality and recovery: listening to the voice of the spirit. *Substance abuse and recovery: Empowerment of deaf persons, conference proceedings.* Washington, DC: College for Continuing Education, The National Academy, Gallaudet University.

Johnstone, M. (1991–92, Winter). The silent majority. *Gallaudet today.*

Kannapell, B.M., Ph.D. (1993). *Language choice — identity choice.* Burtonsville, MD: Linstock Press Dissertation Series, Linstock Press, Inc.

Kannapell, B.M., & Adams, P. (1984). *Orientation to deafness: a handbook and resource guide.* Washington, DC: Gallaudet College.

Lane, H., Hoffmeister, R., & Bahan, B. (1996). *A journey into the Deaf-World.* San Diego: DawnSignPress.

Markowicz, H., & Woodward, J. (1978). Language and the maintenance of ethnic boundaries in the deaf community. *Communication and cognition.*

McCrone, W.P., Ed.D., J.D. (1990, June 5–9). Empowerment through advocacy by deaf people for meaningfully accessible substance abuse/alcoholism treatment. *Substance abuse and recovery: Empowerment of deaf persons, conference proceedings.* Washington, DC: College for Continuing Education, The National Academy, Gallaudet University.

McCrone, W.P., Ed.D., J.D. (1994). Problem #4: drug abuse among deaf job seekers. *JADARA,* (vol. 28, no. 2, Fall, 1994). A journal for professionals networking for excellence in service delivery with individuals who are deaf or hard of hearing.

Mellody, P., & Wells Miller, A. (1989). *Breaking free: A recovery workbook for facing co-dependence.* New York: Harper & Row.

Miller, B.G. Ed.D., CCAC. (1989, May/June). Empowerment: Treatment approaches for the chemically addicted. *The counselor.*

Miller, B.G. Ed.D., CCAC. (1990, June 5–9). Coping strategies for deaf people in recovery. *Substance abuse and recovery: Empowerment of deaf persons, conference proceedings.* Washington, DC: College for Continuing Education, The National Academy, Gallaudet University.

Miller, B.G. Ed.D., CCAC. (1990, June 5–9). Courage to change. A keynote presentation. *Substance abuse and recovery: Empowerment of deaf persons, conference proceedings.* Washington, DC: College for Continuing Education, The National Academy, Gallaudet University.

Miller, B.G. Ed.D., CCAC. (1995, Feb. 24–26). Understanding co-dependency in professional services for deaf persons: A training session for professional helpers. A workshop presented at Soberfest: Deaf Celebration and Challenges, Princeton, NJ. Sponsored by Signs of Sobriety.

Modry, J. (1989, July 9–14). Cultural implications of treating the hearing impaired substance abuser. A presentation for THE DEAF WAY conference, Gallaudet University. Washington, DC.

Myers, K, R.N. (1994, Summer). Co-dependency. *Steps to recovery.*

National directory of alcohol and other drugs prevention and treatment programs accessible to the deaf. (1995). Rochester, NY: Rochester Institute of Technology.

"New life" acceptance program (13 statements). (1993). Quarkertown, PA: Women for Sobriety, Inc.

The next step: A national conference focussing on issues related to substance abuse in the deaf and hard of hearing population, conference proceedings. (1992, July 5–8), College for Continuing Education, National Academy, Gallaudet University, Washington, DC.

Orlandi, M.A., Ph.D., editor, (1992). *Cultural competence for evaluations: A guide for alcohol and other drug abuse prevention practitioners working with ethnic/racial communities.* U.S. Department of Health and Human Services, Public Health Service, Alcohol, Drug Abuse, and Mental Health Administration, Office of Substance Abuse Prevention.

Padden, C, & Humphries, T., (1988). *Deaf in America: Voices from a culture.* Cambridge, MA: Harvard University Press.

Recovery begins with step one. (1997, Winter). *Steps to recovery.*

Rheney, T., M.D., McGuirt, W.F., Jr., & Jewett, T., M.D. (1997, Sept. 16). High incidence of hearing loss and middle ear disease found among children with fetal alcohol syndrome. *In the news*. Winston-Salem, NC: Bowman-Gray School of Medicine.

Sandberg, K. (1996, Nov.). Deaf people and addiction; Barriers to recovery. *The quarterly*.

Schaef, A.W. (1986). *Co-dependence, misunderstood, mistreated*. San Francisco: Harper & Row.

Snider, B.D., editor (1994). *Innovative partnerships in recovery: The diverse deaf experience, conference proceedings*. (1994, Nov. 3–5). Washington, DC.: College for Continuing Education, Gallaudet University.

Solomon, A. (1994, Aug. 28). Defiantly deaf. *The New York times magazine*, Section 6.

Substance abuse and recovery; Empowerment of deaf persons, conference proceedings. (1990, June 5–9). Washington, DC: The National Academy, Gallaudet University.

Twelve steps and twelve traditions. (1973). New York: Alcoholics Anonymous World Services, Inc.

Vernon, M., Ph.D., & Inskip, R. (1988). *The Randy Inskip story*. Silver Spring, MD: National Association of the Deaf Publications.

Watson, D., Steitler, L., Peterson, P., & Fulton, W.K., editors. (1983). *Mental health, substance abuse and deafness*. Silver Spring, MD: American Deafness and Rehabilitation Association.

White, F., Ed.D. (1990, June 5–9). The inheritors: Children of alcoholics. *Substance abuse and recovery: Empowerment of deaf persons, conference proceedings*. Washington, DC: College for Continuing Education, The National Academy, Gallaudet University.

Woititz, J.G., Ed.D. (1985). *Struggle for intimacy*. Pompano Beach, FL: Health Communications, Inc.

Woodward, J. (1972). Implications for sociolinguists research among the deaf. *Sign language studies*.

Index

AA *see* Alcoholics Anonymous

abstinence 9, 172

ACA *see* Adult Children of Alcoholics

ACOA *see* Adult Children of Alcoholics

ADA *see* Americans with Disabilities Act

Adult Children of Alcoholic(s)/ACOA/ACA 1, 10, 19, 116-117, 131-132, 170

advocacy 51, 125-137, 160-167

advocate 10, 25, 57-58, 64, 80-92, 159-167

African-American 23, 29, 39, 44-46, 92

aftercare 24-25, 45-47, 57, 64, 67-94, 128-138, 173-178

Al-Anon 1, 39, 50, 118, 129, 170-171

Ala-Teen 19

Alcoholics Anonymous/AA 1-8, 13, 19-22, 24-25, 35, 38-40, 43-47, 50-51, 67, 95-120, 151, 171, 177

ambivalent 21, 35, 36, 37-38, 40, 150, 154

American Sign Language/ASL 1-2, 12-13, 15-17, 19-23, 25, 28-31, 33, 35, 36-38, 46, 57, 59, 60-65, 91, 95, 142

Americans with Disabilities Act/ADA 64-65, 153-154, 159-168

anger 74, 77, 82, 87-88, 135-136, 148, 157

ASL *see* American Sign Language

assessment 55-61, 80-88

audiological perspective 33

audists 31

Awakenings 58

brain dysfunction 169-178

brain problems 12-26

chemical dependency 8, 88, 171
co-dependent 1, 125-130, 148, 154-155
cocaine 12, 72
code of ethics 41-42, 113-115, 144
confidentiality 39-40, 43, 50, 98, 107, 113, 117, 132, 137, 144-145, 147, 155, 157
crack 12, 23-24, 72
cultural perspective 33
culture 1-5, 10, 13, 16, 25, 28-29, 31-34, 36, 49-50, 147

deaf club(s) 3, 27-31, 33, 43, 46, 52, 63, 90-91, 125-126, 128-129, 135-136
Deaf community 2, 7, 10-11, 16-17, 19-21, 24, 28-52, 58, 60, 63, 65, 70, 74, 78-81, 89-91, 98-100, 103-107, 117-118, 123, 125-131, 136-137, 144-145, 154, 165-166, 169-174
Deaf culture 1-2, 22, 25, 27-52, 59-63, 68-69, 71, 77, 81, 84, 91, 101, 122, 131-135, 143-144, 146-147, 156, 165-166
deaf school(s) 12, 17, 33-34, 37, 44, 75 *see also* residential schools for the deaf
deaf women 47-49
Deaf world 18, 21, 28-29, 38, 52
deafened 14-18, 20-21, 24-25, 28
denial 5, 6, 11, 14, 23, 78-79, 81, 116-117, 125
dependent 13-14, 21, 40, 82-83, 88, 126-127, 130, 135-136
depression 61, 73-74
detoxification center 5-9, 55-57
disability 20-21, 74-75, 163-164
disability community 11
disease 8-9, 25, 47-49, 52, 62-63, 124-125, 171-174
disease concept 8
distrust/don't trust 73, 79, 116 *see also* mistrust
DUI (Driving Under the Influence) 5
DWI (Driving While Intoxicated) 5

empowerment 91, 165-166
English 2, 8, 12, 15, 23, 30-31, 36-38, 41-42, 46, 49, 62, 72, 74, 83, 95-96, 98, 99-100, 102-107, 112, 132, 142-143, 147, 161-162

fetal alcohol syndrome 10

gay 46-47
GLAD *see* Greater Los Angeles Council on Deafness
gossip 11, 29, 40-41, 91, 103, 105, 126, 136
Greater Los Angeles Council on Deafness/GLAD 159-160

grief 16, 73, 177

hard of hearing 6, 14, 15, 17-22, 25, 28-29, 34-35, 58-60, 64-65, 126, 160
hearing impaired 28, 35, 37-38, 133
hearing loss 10, 14-18, 20-21, 37
helpers 40, 98, 125, 127
heroin 7, 12, 72
Hispanic 44

identity 10, 16, 18, 21, 29-38, 44, 60, 88-89, 174
image 42, 52, 121-123
intake 59-62
interpreter 27-28, 30, 34, 41-44, 55, 58-60, 62-65, 95, 97, 99, 108, 112-114, 118, 159-168, 175-178
interpreting 139-157

Law Center *see* National Association of the Deaf Law Center
lesbian 46-48

mainstream(ed) 12, 18, 29, 38, 74, 75, 111, 134-135, 148
marijuana 12, 23
medications 73-94
medicine 72-94

Minnesota Chemical Dependency Program for Deaf and Hard of Hearing Individuals 58
mistrust 40-42, 81, 148, 155 *see also distrust*

NA *see* Narcotics Anonymous
NAD *see* National Association of the Deaf
Narcotics Anonymous/NA 1, 6-8, 13, 24, 27, 39, 44, 47, 50-51, 65, 67 68, 139, 141, 143, 146, 155-156, 164, 171-172
National Association of the Deaf 143-144, 164-165
National Association of the Deaf Law Center 153-154, 164

oppress 19, 25
oppression 19, 30-31, 47
oppressors 40
oral deaf 28
oral interpreters 20
oral interpreting 60
oral method 70
oral schools 12

parents 9-14, 17, 19, 23, 41, 47, 70, 75, 88, 101, 116-117, 163, 165
Registry of Interpreters for the Deaf/RID 143-145

Relay service(s) 67, 83, 99

resentment 21, 24-25, 73-74, 77-78, 90-91, 105-107, 135-136, 157

residential school(s) for the deaf *see also* deaf schools 3, 172

RID *see* Registry of Interpreters for the Deaf

role model(s) 10-11, 36, 50-51, 62, 92, 122-123, 129, 134-135, 165-166, 175

school 11-12, 18-21, 23, 28, 30, 33-34, 36, 38-39, 44-46, 75, 85, 123

Section 504 159-168

shame 5, 6, 11, 19-21, 43, 48, 52, 81, 117-118, 135, 173

sign-gloss 2

signed English 2, 23, 142, 146, 149

signs, use of specific signs for drugs 72

Signs of Recovery/SOR 59, 64, 65

sponsors 65, 87-88, 98-99, 107-111, 167, 176

telephone relay *see* Relay service

treatment program(s) 2-5, 6, 16, 22-25, 42, 45, 48-49, 56- 60, 63, 65, 67-68, 72, 80, 85, 121-137, 141, 143, 147-149, 155, 157, 160-161, 163, 166, 172-173, 175

TRS *see* relay service

trust 5, 7, 25, 40-42, 47, 70-71, 75, 77, 79, 90, 102-103, 108, 116, 122, 132-133, 145, 165-166, 176

12 Step(s) 1, 5, 35, 67, 81, 95-100, 102, 106-108, 110, 129, 146, 159, 160, 166, 170, 175-177

12 Tradition(s) 1, 67, 96, 111, 146

vitamins 71-73

vocational rehabilitation 1, 45, 69